NuWave Oven
COOKBOOK FOR BEGINNERS

Healthy and Delicious NuWave Oven Recipes that Friends and Loved Ones Will Be Begging You to Serve!

Frankie Nicholson

© Copyright 2018 by Frankie Nicholson- All rights reserved.

ISBN: 978-1720566793

This document is geared towards providing exact and reliable information in regard to the topic and issue covered. The publication is sold with the idea that the publisher is not required to render accounting, officially permitted, or otherwise, qualified services. If advice is necessary, legal or professional, a practiced individual in the profession should be ordered.

From a Declaration of Principles which was accepted and approved equally by a Committee of the American Bar Association and a Committee of Publishers and Associations.

In no way is it legal to reproduce, duplicate, or transmit any part of this document in either electronic means or in printed format. Recording of this publication is strictly prohibited and any storage of this document is not allowed unless with written permission from the publisher. All rights reserved.

The information provided herein is stated to be truthful and consistent, in that any liability, in terms of inattention or otherwise, by any usage or abuse of any policies, processes, or directions contained within is the solitary and utter responsibility of the recipient reader. Under no circumstances will any legal responsibility or blame be held against the publisher for any reparation, damages, or monetary loss due to the information herein, either directly or indirectly.

Respective authors own all copyrights not held by the publisher.

Contents

Introduction 4

Chapter 1
NuWave Oven Offers Multiple Benefits! 5

Chapter 2
Breakfast Recipes 8

Chapter 3
Snacks & Appetizers 20

Chapter 4
Poultry-Based NuWave Oven Recipes 34

Chapter 5
Beef, Lamb & Pork-Based Recipes 53

Chapter 6
Vegetable-Based NuWave Oven Recipes 81

Chapter 7
Desserts 94

Conclusion 99

Introduction

This is a collection of healthy and tasty recipes that you can quickly prepare with your NuWave Oven. The NuWave Oven is a multi-purpose kitchen appliance that sits on your countertop, offering three styles of heat—convection, infrared, and conduction. This unique combination results in saving a whole lot of time and energy while at the same time trims extra fats and calories from your foods.

No need to worry about preheating your foods with your NuWave Oven, nor will you have to defrost foods before placing them in the oven. You can simply take frozen foods and put them directly from the freezer into this extraordinary appliance. Quickly set the time and heat, then sit back and relax while your new appliance does all the arduous work of preparing your foods! You will have more time to spend doing the things you love to do—such as having more one-on-one time with loved ones! You can feel good knowing that you are healthily preparing your foods, as you will no longer need to use any extra fat while cooking your food in your new NuWave Oven!

Chapter 1
NuWave Oven Offers Multiple Benefits!

The new method of NuWave Oven cooking with its 3 different types of heat production can help you prepare your foods more efficiently. Below are listed some benefits you will gain when using a NuWave Oven.

Healthy and Delicious Cooking:

The NuWave Oven, as mentioned before, operates with a triple combination cooking power to cook your foods. This cooking method is powerful in that it removes all the extra fat from your food, in the form of fat drippings. The food remains juicy and tender on the inside.

It also offers a faster cooking cycle. This impressive appliance makes sure that the nutritional value of your food is not lost because of excessive heating for several hours. The result is that you have a plate of food that is low in fat but is juicy, and it still has most of its nutrients undamaged.

Seafood & Meats Come out Simply Mouth-watering:

With the use of the NuWave Oven, you can prepare many different food items, from meat to poultry, to vegetables, to seafood of all types. You can cook poultry whole or in parts, and it will turn out tender and succulent with a perfectly golden-brownish exterior. Fish prepared in the NuWave Oven has a nice flaky interior with a crispy exterior.

Save Precious Time:

An excellent feature of the NuWave Oven is its time saving ability, and we all know how precious our time is. With this appliance, you will not need to pre-heat it in advance. This alone will easily save you 20 minutes (which you may have spent watching your oven while you waited for it to reach the correct temperature). Place the food into your NuWave Oven, and it will be cooked immediately!

Another fantastic time saver is that you do not have to spend time waiting for frozen foods to defrost. You can take frozen foods from the freezer and place them directly into your NuWave Oven, set the temperature, and you are all set!

Re-heat with Ease:

Imagine your NuWave oven will not only re-heat food, but it will breathe new life into it. Picture re-heating some refrigerated fried chicken breast leftovers. The extra fat drips away, leaving you with a beautiful piece of fat-free, crispy chicken to enjoy.

Power Saver:

When you are preparing your meals using your NuWave Oven, not only are you creating tasty, healthy meals, but you are also doing your part to save our planet. How? Let me explain this precious bonus! You will firstly save a lot of energy using your NuWave Oven in place of your regular oven. A huge 2/3 of the energy that would be used using your conventional oven is used by the NuWave Oven. Simply, it does not waste energy pre-heating. When using a conventional oven, you need to preheat it so it achieves the desired temperature you are seeking.

Tips and Tricks to use when Cooking with Your NuWave Oven

- You cannot simply bake and grill in your NuWave Oven; you can toast several different pieces of bread, muffins, or bagels inside it as well. All you must do is place the selection of bread on the 4-inch rack on high, and you will have thoroughly toasted bread within 4 minutes.

- Make sure you always have your oven mitts on when you using your Nuwave Oven. Your NuWave Oven will get hot and can scald your palms and fingers if you are not careful.

- Using the multi-level cooking function is easy and fun to use. Just keep in mind that foods usually do not take the same amount of time to cook. Therefore, make sure to place the foods that take longer to cook on the lower rack and the faster cooking foods on higher racks.

- Clean your NuWave Oven after each use. If you do not clean it, then the previous leftovers could end up burning and sticking in your oven, which will make the clean up a much messier ordeal.

- To aid in the cleaning of the fat drippings, place a heavy-duty aluminum foil on the Linear Pan. When you are done cooking, you can lift the foil out of the pan without having to scrub the pan!

- Make sure the dome of the oven is cooled completely before you remove the power head from your NuWave Oven.

- Make sure your NuWave Oven is turned off when you clean it and is cooled and unplugged.
- When you clean your NuWave Oven, do not use rough pads or chemical cleaners on it, as they might cause damage to the surface of your oven. It is also suggested that you manually clean all the enamel racks and do not put them in the dishwasher.

NuWave Oven Temperature Conversion Guide

Oven Temperature in Fahrenheit	Oven Temperature in Celsius	Power Level
106° Fahrenheit	41° Celsius	1
116° Fahrenheit	47° Celsius	2
150° Fahrenheit	66° Celsius	3
175° Fahrenheit	79° Celsius	4
225° Fahrenheit	107° Celsius	5
250° Fahrenheit	121° Celsius	6
275° Fahrenheit	135° Celsius	7
300° Fahrenheit	149° Celsius	8
325° Fahrenheit	163° Celsius	9
342° Fahrenheit	172° Celsius	10 (HI)

Conversions Chart

Unit:	Equals:	Also Equals:
1 teaspoon	⅓ tablespoon	¼ fluid ounce
1 tablespoon	3 teaspoons	½ fluid ounce
⅛ cup	2 tablespoons	1 fluid ounce
¼ cup	4 tablespoons	2 fluid ounces
1/3 cup	¼ cup plus 4 teaspoons	2 ¾ fluid ounces
½ cup	8 tablespoons	4 fluid ounces
1 cup	½ pint	8 fluid ounces
1 pint	2 cups	16 fluid ounces
1 quart	4 cups	32 fluid ounces
1 liter	1 quart plus ¼ cup	4 ¼ cups
1 gallon	4 quarts	16 cups

Chapter 2
Breakfast Recipes

YUMMY BREKKIE MUFFINS

Preparation time: 5 minutes | Cook time: 20 minutes | Servings: 6

Ingredients:

- 2 ounces of butter
- 1 ¼ cup self-raising flour
- 1 egg, lightly beaten
- ½ cup diced tomato, seeded
- ½ cup grated cheese
- 2 slices crispy bacon, chopped
- ½ teaspoon paprika
- ½ cup buttermilk

Instructions:

1. Sift the flour into mixing bowl.
2. Add the melted butter, milk, egg, and paprika and mix well.
3. Add cheese, tomato, and bacon to mixture and stir to blend.
4. Fill six silicone muffin cups and bake in the NuWave oven on 1-inch rack on high (342° F) for 20 minutes and serve muffins warm.

Nutritional Information per serving:

Calories: 382, Total Fat: 12.2g, Carbs: 8.9g, , Protein: 14.8g

TASTY STUFFED BANANA FRENCH TOAST

Preparation time: 35 minutes | Cook time: 30 minutes | Servings: 4

Ingredients:

4 slices of French bread, cut into 1-inch slices, with crusts removed

2 bananas, peeled and sliced diagonally

3 eggs, beaten

2 ounces butter

Zest of 1 orange

1 tablespoon orange liqueur

1 teaspoon vanilla extract

½ cup half and half milk/cream

Instructions:

1. Cut a slice through each piece of bread, leaving the bottom intact to create a pocket and fill it with slices of banana. Pack firmly into the greased pan in single layer. I like using a square cake tin for this.

2. In a mixing bowl, beat eggs, vanilla extract, milk/cream, orange liqueur, and orange zest.

3. Add this mixture to the bread slices in the pan and allow to rest for 30 minutes.

4. Bake in NuWave Oven on 2-inch rack for 30 minutes. Serve with yogurt.

Nutritional Information per serving:

Calories: 427, Total Fat: 14.2g, Carbs: 9.7g, Protein: 11.5g

MINI CRUST-LESS QUICHE

Preparation time: 10 minutes | Cook time: 25 minutes | Servings: 12

Ingredients:

6 large eggs

1 lb. mixed bell peppers, seeded and diced

1 teaspoon kosher salt

½ teaspoon ground black pepper

½ cup heavy cream

6 large egg yolks

½ cup whole milk

Instructions:

1. Crack the eggs into a mixing bowl. Add cream, egg yolks, pepper, salt, and milk and whisk to combine. Whisk until light and fluffy.

2. Pour the egg mixture into a jar and set aside.

3. Place 12 silicon muffin liners on the rack and spray them with cooking spray.

4. Divide half of the peppers equally among the muffin liners.

5. Pour the egg mixture over peppers.

6. Bake the quiches for 25 minutes on "Hi" setting at 342°Fahrenheit.

7. Cool the quiches in the liners for a few minutes before unmolding.

8. Repeat the process with remaining batter and bell peppers until done.

9. Serve hot.

Nutritional Information per serving:

Calories: 462, Total Fat: 15.2g, Carbs: 12.3g, Protein: 18.4g

SAUSAGE & EGG BREAKFAST PUDDING

Preparation time: 5 minutes | Cook time: 63 minutes | Servings: 2

Ingredients:

2 mushrooms, sliced

1 tablespoon olive oil

¼ cup leek, sliced

1 green onion, chopped

2 eggs

Sea salt to taste

Fresh ground black pepper to taste

2 cups Hawaiian bread, diced into 1-inch cubes

⅓ cup milk

½ cup Gouda cheese, shredded

½ cup heavy cream

1 cup turkey breakfast sausage, diced

Instructions:

1. Mix olive oil, turkey sausage, mushrooms, and onions in a 10-inch baking pan.

2. Season with sea salt and black pepper.

3. Place the prepared baking pan on the 3-inch cooking rack and cook for 12 minutes at 300° Fahrenheit. Stop the oven 5 minutes into cook time to stir and ensure even cooking.

4. While the sausage mixture is baking, place the milk, eggs, heavy cream and Gouda cheese in a mixing bowl and whisk well.

5. Once sausage mix is done cooking, leave baking pan in oven to rest.

6. Add bread cubes to the egg mixture and mix well.

7. Remove your sausage mix from oven and pour the egg mixture over it and mix well.

8. Place pan back into the oven on the 1-inch cooking rack and bake for 50 minutes at 300° Fahrenheit.

9. Allow the dish to rest after cooked in the oven for a few minutes before serving.

10. Top with fresh herbs when serving.

Nutritional Information per serving:

Calories: 462, Total Fat: 11.4g, Carbs: 17.8g, Protein: 22.3g

CHOPPED BACON OMELETS

Preparations: 5 minutes | Cook time: 15 minutes | Servings: 3

Ingredients:

5 eggs

½ cup beef bacon, chopped into bite-size pieces

¼ cup milk

3-ounces cheddar cheese, shredded

⅛ cup onion, chopped

¼ cup green pepper, chopped

½ tablespoon parsley, chopped

Instructions:

1. Add to a mixing bowl eggs and milk, whisk until fluffy.
2. Add the cheese, beef bacon, green pepper, and onion, mix well.
3. Pour the egg and meat mixture in a 4-inch by 4-inch silicon baking dish sprayed with cooking spray.
4. Place the baking dish on the 1-inch rack. Set the temperature to "High" (342°Fahrenheit) setting and bake for 15 minutes. Let the eggs sit in the dome with the heat off for a minute.
5. Remove the egg from baking dish and cut into pieces.
6. Serve hot with a side of baked English muffins or whole bread.

Nutritional Information per serving:
Calories: 367, Total Fat: 15.2g, Carbs: 8.4g, Protein: 17.2g

STEAK, STUFFED TOMATO WITH CHEESE & EGGS

Preparation time: 5 minutes | Cook time: 10 minutes | Servings: 2

Ingredients:

2 (4-ounce) sirloin steaks

2 scallions, thinly sliced

2 tablespoons butter

4 large eggs

4 tablespoons Parmesan cheese, grated

Salt and pepper to taste

1 tomato, cut in half and seeds removed

Instructions:

1. Crack open the eggs into a shallow, ovenproof baking dish.
2. Break the yolks carefully and place the dish on the liner pan.
3. Slice the rounded side of tomato in half so they can stand on the bottom.
4. Stuff the tomato halves with grated cheese.
5. Add salt and pepper to steak using fingers to rub it in.

6. Place the stuffed tomato halves and steak on the 3-inch rack.

7. Set your NuWave Oven to the "High" setting (342°Fahrenheit) and bake for 10 minutes for a medium steak. Cut the egg into two halves.

9. On two serving plates evenly divide steaks, cheese stuffed tomato halves, and eggs between them. Serve with some toast.

Nutrition Information per serving:

Calories: 443, Total Fat: 11.2g, Carbs: 8.7g, Protein: 13.2g

BREAKFAST CHEESE FRITTATA

Preparation time: 5 minutes | Cook time: 23 minutes | Servings: 2

Ingredients:

- ½ cup ricotta
- 1 ½ cups of pasta (any kind)
- 8 slices bacon
- ¼ cup tomato sauce
- ½ tablespoon olive oil
- ½ cup Parmesan cheese, grated
- 2 large eggs

Instructions:

1. Place the bacon slices on a 4-inch cooking rack in a single layer. Cook on "High" setting (342° Fahrenheit) for 8 minutes.

2. Remove the bacon slices from your oven, allow them to cool then crumble them.

3. Combine the ricotta, Parmesan, eggs, bacon crumble, tomato sauce, olive oil, and pasta in a mixing bowl. Mix well to combine.

4. Lightly grease a large baking dish with some butter or cooking spray.

5. Pour the prepared pasta mixture into the pan and use the back of a spoon to press the mix into the bottom of the pan.

6. Place pan on the 4-inch cooking rack and bake for 15 minutes.

7. During the last 7 minutes of baking cover the top of the pan with a piece of foil to prevent over-browning. Add to large serving bowl and serve hot.

Nutritional Information per serving:

Calories: 462, Total Fat: 16.2g, Carbs: 9.3g, Protein: 19.2g

BREAKFAST BISCUITS

Preparation time: 5 minutes | Cooking time: 17 minutes | Servings: 6

Ingredients:

- 1 large ripe banana
- ½ teaspoon baking soda
- ½ cup whole wheat plain flour
- 1 cup plain flour
- 2 egg whites
- ¼ cup water
- ¾ cup granulated sugar
- ¾ cup peanut butter
- ½ teaspoon salt
- 2 cups quick-cooking rolled oats
- ½ cup chopped walnuts
- ¼ cup chocolate chips

Instructions:

1. In a mixing bowl, mash the banana. Using an electric mixer, beat in the peanut butter, sugar, water, and egg whites until smooth.

2. Add sifted flour, baking soda, and salt.

3. Add the remaining ingredients, stirring to combine.

4. Using tablespoons of mixture, roll into a ball. Flatten the balls with palms of hands and place on 2-inch rack.

5. Bake at 342° Fahrenheit in your NuWave Oven for 15 minutes, turn over and bake for an additional 2 minutes. Give biscuits time to cool on a wire rack.

Nutritional Information per serving:

Calories: 422, Total Fat: 9.2g, Carbs: 7.4g, Protein: 8.4g

CRUNCHY FRENCH TOAST

Preparation time: 5 minutes | Cook time: 15 minutes | Servings: 4

Ingredients:

½ cup corn flakes, crumbled

½ (16-ounce) container of egg substitute

¼ loaf of bread (any type), sliced into thick slices

Instructions:

1. Pour the egg substitute into a shallow baking pan.

2. Add the slices of bread into the egg substitute and soak for a minute or so.

3. Place the crumbled cornflakes in a flat dish and coat the egg substitute-soaked bread with the crumbled cornflakes.

4. Place the bread slices on the 3-inch rack and bake on the "High" setting (342° Fahrenheit) for about 15 minutes.

5. Let bread cool a bit before serving with a side of fresh fruit.

Nutritional Information per serving:

Calories: 387, Total Fat: 8.2g, Carbs: 9.5g, Protein: 6.5g

CHEESY ASPARAGUS FRITTATAS

Preparation time: 5 minutes | Cook time: 60 minutes | Servings: 4

Ingredients:

1 small carrot, peeled, trimmed and finely grated

¼ teaspoon freshly ground black pepper

½ teaspoon salt

½ cup self-raising flour

½ cup milk

6 eggs, lightly beaten

1 small yellow onion, peeled and chopped

10 spears fresh asparagus, trimmed

1 cup white cheddar, grated, divided into ¼, ¼, & ½

½ teaspoon chives, coarsely chopped

½ teaspoon butter

Instructions:

1. Grease a 6-cup Bundt pan with some butter and set aside.

2. Combine about ¼ cup of the grated white cheddar and ¼ teaspoon chives together in a small bowl and set aside.

3. Salt a large pot of water generously and heat over a high flame until bubbling. Lower the heat to a medium-low and add in the asparagus spears.

4. Continue heating on a high flame for about 5 minutes.

5. Drain the asparagus spears from water and place them under cold running water until they are cool enough for you to handle.

6. Pat the asparagus dry using a paper towel.

7. Chop the asparagus spears into 1/4-inch pieces and place the asparagus pieces in a large bowl.

8. Add in the remaining ¼-cup grated white cheddar cheese, onions, flour, salt, eggs, carrots, milk, and pepper to the bowl containing the asparagus and mix well.

9. Pour the prepared mix into the greased Bundt pan and place it on the 1-inch rack in your NuWave Oven.

10. Bake on the "High" setting for 55 minutes or until firm.

11. Once done, allow the Bundt pan to cool until it is manageable to invert the frittatas onto a plate.

12. Sprinkle the remaining ½ cup grated cheese and remaining ¼ teaspoon of chives on the frittatas.

13. Return the frittatas to the Bundt pan and place on the 1-inch rack.

14. Bake on "High" setting (342° Fahrenheit) for 3 minutes or until the cheese melts.

15. Serve hot!

Nutritional Information per serving:

Calories: 373, Total Fat: 11.2g, Carbs: 7.6g, Protein: 8.2g

CORN & BACON BREAKFAST PIZZA

Preparation time: 10 minutes | Cook time: 10 minutes | Servings: 2

Ingredients:

- 1 large round pita bread
- 1 tablespoon corn relish
- 1 tablespoon fresh flat-leaf parsley, coarsely chopped
- ¼ cup of mixed mozzarella, parmesan cheese
- 1 rasher of bacon, finely chopped

Instructions:

1. Spread pita bread with relish. Top with bacon and cheese.
2. Cook in NuWave Oven on 4-inch rack at 342° Fahrenheit for 10 minutes.
3. Sprinkle with parsley just before serving.

Nutritional Information per serving:

Calories: 378, Total Fat: 9.2g, Carbs: 6.4g, Protein: 15.7g

VEGEMITE SCROLLS & CHEESE

Preparation time: 10 minutes | Cooking time: 12 minutes | Servings: 6

Ingredients:

- 3 cups self-raising flour
- 2 cups milk
- Pinch of salt
- 1 ½ ounces butter
- 2 tablespoons vegemite
- 7 ounces cheese, shredded
- 2 tablespoons parmesan cheese (mix with tasty cheese)

Instructions:

1. Sift flour along with salt into a bowl, then rub through butter (alternatively, process flour and butter in a food processor).

2. Stir in just enough milk to make the dough soft. Knead dough gently on a lightly floured surface to form a 15-inch by 10-inch rectangle.

3. Spread the Vegemite over your dough, then sprinkle ¾ of the cheese over it. Roll up along the long side to enclose the cheese. Cut into 4-inch by 1 ½ inches from the roll and place close together, with cut side up on 1-inch rack.

4. Sprinkle with your remaining cheese and bake at 342° Fahrenheit in your NuWave Oven for 10 minutes, then turn over and bake for an additional 2 minutes.

Nutritional Information per serving:

Calories: 422, Total Fat: 13.2g, Carbs: 9.4g, Protein: 8.2g

HAM & EGGS SCRAMBLE

Preparation time: 5 minutes | Cook time: 9 minutes | Servings: 2

Ingredients:

4 large eggs

4 ounces cheddar cheese, shredded

6 ounces ham, chopped

Pepper and salt to taste

¼ cup parsley, fresh, chopped

Instructions:

1. Add all the ingredients into a baking dish and mix well.

2. Place the dish in your NuWave Oven on the 3-inch rack.

3. Bake at 375° Fahrenheit and set timer for 7 minutes on "High" power level.

4. Stir and bake for an additional 2-minutes.

Nutritional Information per serving:

Calories: 342, Total Fat: 17.2g, Carbs: 11.3g, Protein: 18.2g

GRILLED CHEESE

Preparation time: 5 minutes | Cook time: 4 minutes | Servings: 8

Ingredients:

8 slices whole wheat bread

4 tablespoons margarine or butter

8 slices American cheese

Instructions:

1. Spread butter on both the sides of bread. Place 4 slices of bread onto the 4-inch rack. Place a cheese slice over it. Cover with remaining bread slices with the buttered side facing up.

2. Select power level "High" at 375° Fahrenheit and grill for about 4 minutes on each side. Serve hot.

Nutritional Information per serving:

Calories: 324, Total Fat: 12.2g, Carbs: 8.7g, Protein: 14.3g

CHORIZO SAUSAGE & EGGS

Preparation time: 5 minutes | Cook time: 10 minutes | Servings: 4

Ingredients:

12 ounces chorizo sausage

8 ounces Monterey Jack cheese, shredded

8 tablespoons salsa

8 large eggs

Instructions:

1. Place the sausage on a saucer and press around the edges. Repeat with remaining sausages.

2. Break 2 eggs in the middle of each sausage. Spoon salsa on top and cheese on top.

3. Place them on the 1-inch rack and cook on "High" power level at 375° Fahrenheit and set the timer for 10 minutes.

Nutritional Information per serving:

Calories: 422, Total Fat: 14.2g, Carbs: 11.2g, Protein: 13.4g

Chapter 3
Snacks & Appetizers

SWEET & SOUR COCKTAIL MEATBALLS

Preparation time: 10 minutes | Cook time: 23 minutes | Servings: 10

Ingredients:

¼ teaspoon red pepper flakes

1 ½ tablespoons Worcestershire sauce

1 ¼ cups apricot preserve

1 small onion, minced

1 clove garlic, minced

1 ¼ lbs. lean ground beef

¼ lbs. ground pork

¼ cup milk

1 tablespoon Dijon mustard

2 tablespoons brown sugar

14 ounce can tomato sauce

2 teaspoons vegetable oil

1 teaspoon pepper

½ teaspoon salt

¼ cup fresh parsley, finely chopped

2 slices bread, torn

1 large egg

Instructions:

1. Add egg, milk, and bread in a bowl. Mash with a fork until well combined.
2. Add pork, parsley, garlic, pepper, and salt and mix well.
3. Add beef and mix well, using your hands.
4. Make small balls about 1 ¼ inch in diameter.

5. Lay the meatballs on the 3-inch rack.

6. Bake for 8 minutes per side at 350° Fahrenheit.

7. Meanwhile, add rest of the ingredients into a saucepan and stir.

8. Place saucepan over medium heat and allow to simmer for 15 minutes.

9. Add the meatballs into sauce and mix until they are well coated.

10. Transfer onto a serving platter. Insert toothpicks and serve hot.

Nutritional Information per serving:
Calories: 423, Total Fat: 16.2g, Carbs: 11.5g, Protein: 18.7g

BEEF KABOBS

Preparation time: 10 minutes | Cook time: 12 minutes | Servings: 8

Ingredients:

4 onions, quartered

32 pieces of lean ground beef top round or sirloin steak, boneless about 3 lbs.

16 small mushrooms

32 pieces of pineapple chunks

For marinade:

1 cup soy sauce

4 tablespoons lemon juice

4 teaspoons garlic, minced

½ cup water

4 tablespoons honey

6 tablespoons green onions, thinly sliced

Instructions:

1. Blend the ingredients for the marinade together in a bowl. Add the beef and mix well.

2. Cover and refrigerate for about 8 hours. Stir a few times during the marinating.

3. Remove the bowl from the fridge 30 minutes before cooking.

4. Drain the liquid from the beef and set aside.

5. Take the skewers, metal or wooden. If wooden, soak for 30 minutes in a large bowl of water.

6. Thread the pineapple, mushroom, onion, and beef onto skewers as you like.

7. Place the skewers on the 4-inch rack. Baste with the drained marinade that was set aside.

8. Cook on the "High" level of power setting at 375° Fahrenheit and set the timer for 6 minutes.

9. Turn the skewers around and baste again and cook for an additional 6 minutes.

Nutritional Information per serving:
Calories: 463, Total Fat: 14.2g, Carbs: 8.7g, Protein: 22.1g

DEVILLED EGGS

Preparation time: 10 minutes | Cook time: 12 minutes | Servings: 8

Ingredients:

2 teaspoons yellow mustard

8 large eggs

Salt and pepper to taste

1 teaspoon paprika

½ cup mayonnaise or miracle whip

5 tablespoons sweet pickle, diced

1 ½ tablespoons apple cider vinegar

Instructions:

1. Place the eggs on the 4-inch rack. Cook them on "High" power level at 350° F with the timer set for 12 minutes.

2. Cool the eggs for 5 minutes in the oven with the dome on.

3. Remove the eggs and place them in a bowl of chilled water. Peel and halve the eggs.

4. Gently remove the yolks from eggs and place into small mixing bowl. Mash yolks.

5. Add vinegar, sweet pickles, salt, pepper, miracle whip and mix well.

6. Fill the white cavities of the eggs with yolk mixture. Sprinkle tops with paprika, place on a serving platter and serve.

Nutritional Information per serving:

Calories: 312, Total Fat: 11.2g, Carbs: 7.6g, Protein: 13.2g

STUFFED MUSHROOMS

Preparation time: 10 minutes | Cook time: 33 minutes | Servings: 18

Ingredients:

18 large button mushrooms, discard stems

Salt and pepper to taste

1 ½ cups mozzarella cheese, shredded

½ teaspoon sage, fresh and finely chopped

3 stalks celery, finely chopped

3 tablespoons olive oil, divided

3 cloves garlic, minced

1 ½ lbs Italian sausage

Instructions:

1. Add half the oil to the liner pan. Place the sausage in the pan.

2. Cook on "High" power level at 342° Fahrenheit and set timer for 8 minutes.

3. Chop the mushroom stems off and discard. Add garlic along with chopped mushrooms into pan and cook for a few minutes then set aside to cool.

4. In a bowl, add the cheese, celery, sage, salt, pepper, and onion and mix well.

5. Add mushroom caps and remaining oil into another bowl and toss well.

6. Stuff the mushrooms with cheese/sausage mixture. Place the mushroom caps on the 3-inch rack. Cook on "High" power level and set the timer for 25 minutes. Serve warm.

Nutritional Information per serving:

Calories: 304, Total Fat: 9.2g, Carbs: 6.3g, Protein: 15.7g

STUFFED JALAPENOS

Preparation time: 10 minutes | Cook time: 10 minutes | Servings: 20

Ingredients:

- 20 green medium size jalapeno peppers, halved, seeded, discard membranes
- 40 strips bacon, soft cooked
- 2 teaspoons oregano
- 2 teaspoons paprika
- 2 lbs. ground pork
- 40 toothpicks, soaked in water

Instructions:

1. Mix all the ingredients except for pepper halves and bacon in a bowl.
2. Stuff this mixture into pepper halves.
3. Wrap a strip of bacon around each half of pepper and secure with a toothpick.
4. Place on 3-inch rack in your NuWave Oven. Place a piece of foil below the rack. Bake in batches. Bake at 350° Fahrenheit and set the timer for 10 minutes.
5. Take out of your NuWave Oven and cool for 5 minutes before serving.

Nutritional Information per serving:

Calories: 312, Total Fat: 11.2g, Carbs: 7.3g, Protein: 14.2g

TOASTED PITA CHIPS WITH GARLIC & ARTICHOKE DIP

Preparation time: 14 minutes | Cook time: 16 minutes | Servings: 12

Ingredients:

- ½ package of fresh pita chips
- ¼ cup parsley, finely chopped
- ⅛ cup olive oil
- ⅛ cup parmesan cheese
- Salt and pepper to taste
- ¼ cup breadcrumbs
- ¼ cup mayonnaise
- ½ cup heavy cream
- 1 tablespoon fresh garlic, minced
- 2 cups Monterey Jack cheese, shredded and also divided
- ½ (12-ounce) can medium diced artichokes, drained

Instructions:

1. Combine the diced artichokes, 1-cup Monterey Jack cheese, cream, breadcrumbs, pepper, garlic, mayonnaise, parmesan cheese and salt in mixing bowl. Mix until ingredients are well combined.

2. Pour the mixture into the large 10-inch baking pan and even the top out using the back of a spatula.

3. Top with the remaining Monterey Jack cheese.

4. Place the baking dish on the 1-inch rack and bake on "High" power level at 350°Fahrenheit for 12 minutes.

5. While the dip cooks, cut the pita bread into 6 pieces per slice.

6. Place the pita chips in a bowl and pour the olive oil over them. Toss to coat.

7. Place the chips on the 4-inch cooking rack in a single layer and toast for about 4 minutes on "High" power level at 350° Fahrenheit.

8. Place the toasted pita chips in a bowl, top with parsley, pepper, parmesan cheese, and salt.

9. Serve immediately with the prepared dip on the side.

Nutritional Information per serving:
Calories: 422, Total Fat: 8.3g, Carbs: 6.4g, Protein: 9.3g

CARAMEL GLAZE CHICKEN SKEWERS

Preparation time: 10 minutes | Cook time: 25 minutes | Servings: 4

Ingredients:

1 tablespoon fish sauce

⅛ cup white sesame seeds

⅛ cup black sesame seeds

⅛ cup almonds, sliced

4 bamboo skewers

1 ¾ lbs. chicken breasts, skinless, cut into 1-inch chunks

1 tablespoon brown sugar

½ tablespoon orange juice

Ingredients for caramel glaze:

⅛ cup fish sauce

1 shallot, chopped

½-inch piece of fresh ginger, minced

½ tablespoon garlic, minced

1 tablespoon honey

⅛ cup orange juice

⅛ cup rice wine vinegar

⅓ cup light brown sugar

Instructions:

1. In a mixing bowl, whisk the fish sauce, brown sugar, and orange juice together with wire whisk.

2. Place the bamboo skewers in some warm water to soak for about six hours.

3. Add the chicken pieces on to the skewers.

4. Place the skewers in a large bowl and pour the prepared marinade over them. Toss to coat. Cover the bowl before putting it in the fridge for 3 hours.

5. In another mixing bowl, combine remaining fish sauce, orange juice, brown sugar, rice wine vinegar, honey, garlic, ginger, and shallot. Whisk to combine.

6. Combine the almonds and sesame seeds and spread an even layer on the bottom of pizza pan.

7. Place the pizza liner pan on the 3-inch cooking rack, toast for 5 minutes at 350° Fahrenheit, and set aside.

8. Place the marinated chicken skewers on the 3-inch cooking rack and lightly brush the prepared caramel glaze over them.

9. Bake for 10 minutes at 350° Fahrenheit.

10. Flip the chicken skewers over and brush some caramel glaze over them. Bake for an additional 10 minutes.

11. Put the prepared skewers on a serving platter and serve hot topped with prepared toasted almonds and sesame seeds.

Nutritional Information per serving:

Calories: 432, Total Fat: 16.2g, Carbs: 9.7g, Protein: 23g

HERB CHEESE FRIES

Preparation time: 12 minutes | Cook time: 17 minutes | Servings: 4

Ingredients:

- 1 lb. frozen fries
- ¼ teaspoon black pepper
- ½ tablespoon rosemary, fresh chopped
- ½ tablespoon oregano, fresh chopped
- ½ tablespoon thyme, fresh chopped
- ½ lb. 3-cheese blend, shredded
- Salt to taste

Instructions:

1. Place the fresh thyme, rosemary, oregano, black pepper, and salt into a small mixing bowl. Mix to combine.

2. Place the frozen fries in a large mixing bowl and pour olive oil over the frozen fries. Toss to coat fries with olive oil.

3. Pour the seasoning mix over the fries and toss to coat.

4. Place the seasoning coated fries on the 3-inch rack in an even layer.

5. Set your NuWave Oven on "High" power level at 342° Fahrenheit and bake for 10 minutes.

6. Once the fries have a crispy exterior, open the dome of your NuWave Oven and transfer the fries from the 3-inch rack to liner pan.

7. Top fries with shredded cheese blend and bake for 7 minutes on "High" setting.

8. When fries are done, open the dome of the oven to allow excess moisture to be released, and the fries will remain crispy and serve hot.

Nutritional Information per serving:

Calories: 432, Total Fat: 12.2g, Carbs: 8.6g, Protein: 9.2g

GOAT CHEESE & WALNUT, PEAR CROSTINI

Preparation time: 12 minutes | Cook time: 11 minutes | Servings: 1

Ingredients:

1 (6-inch) baguette

¼ cup walnuts, coarsely chopped

½ tablespoon brown sugar

½ tablespoon honey plus 1 teaspoon of honey

1 large Bosc pear, peeled, cored and cut lengthwise into wedges about ½-inch thick

½ tablespoon olive oil

3 ounces goat cheese

Extra-virgin olive oil

½ cup basil or arugula (optional)

Sea salt as needed

Instructions:

1. Place the walnuts in a small mixing bowl. Add one teaspoon of honey and brown sugar. Toss to coat walnuts.

2. Put the walnuts in the liner pan in single layer. Place the 3-inch rack over the walnut filled liner pan.

3. Slice the baguette into ½-inch thick slices and arrange on the 3-inch rack in a single layer.

4. Lightly brush olive oil over the baguette slices.

5. Set your NuWave Oven on "High" setting at 350° Fahrenheit and toast baguette for 5 minutes.

6. Remove the bread covered 3-inch rack from oven and toast the walnuts for an additional 6 minutes.

7. Add the toasted bread slices on a flat surface and arrange the pear wedges on the bread in a single layer. Spread the goat cheese on the pears.

8. Top the cheese with the toasted walnuts and garnish with some basil or arugula.

9. Lightly pour some olive oil and honey over the crostini and season to taste with a pinch of sea salt.

10. Rest the crostini for about 30 minutes before serving. This will help to enhance the cheese flavor in the crostini.

11. Serve with a side of toasted walnuts.

Nutritional Information per serving:
Calories: 386, Total Fat: 11.2g, Carbs: 8.4g, Protein: 6.2g

SOUR CREAM & RANCH STUFFED POTATO BITES

Preparation time: 5 minutes | Cook time: 60 minutes | Servings: 8

Ingredients:

Green onions chopped for garnish

Bacon pieces chopped for garnish

2 cups cheddar cheese shredded

½ cup low-fat sour cream

2 packets ranch seasoning

4 medium baked potatoes

Instructions:

1. Place the potatoes on the 1-inch rack and lightly pinch (pinchar) with a fork. Bake them on the "High" setting at 375° Fahrenheit for 50 minutes.

2. Take your potatoes out of the oven and allow to cool for 10 minutes.

3. Cut the potatoes into halves, lengthwise, and use a spoon to scoop out the filling from the skin.

4. Place the potato in mixing bowl. Add in the seasoning mix and low-fat sour cream. Mix well to combine.

5. Spoon the prepared mixture into the skins and top with cheese.

6. Place the prepared skins on the 3-inch rack and bake on "High" setting at 350° Fahrenheit for 10 minutes.

7. Top with bacon bit and green onions and serve immediately.

Nutritional Information per serving:
Calories: 422, Total Fat: 12.2g, Carbs: 9.6g, Protein: 6.2g

TOASTED BACON & GRILLED CHEESE, APPLE SANDWICHES

Preparation time: 10 minutes | Cook time: 9 minutes | Servings: 8

Ingredients:

- 4 tablespoons butter softened
- 8 slices sourdough bread
- 12 ounces smoked Gouda cheese, sliced
- 2 crisp honey apples, cored, sliced
- Salt to taste

Instructions:

1. Apply about ½ a tablespoon of butter on one side of the sourdough bread slice.
2. With the buttered slice up, place the four slices of buttered bread on the 3-inch rack.
3. Toast the bread on "High" setting at 350° Fahrenheit for 4 minutes.
4. Flip the bread over and place 3 strips of bacon and 1 slice of cheese on each slice of bread.
5. Add your apple slices in a single layer over the cheese.
6. Place the remaining buttered slices over the apple slices with their buttered side up.
7. Toast the sandwiches for another 5 minutes on the "High" setting at 350° Fahrenheit.
8. Once toasted, remove the toasted sandwiches on a cutting board and slice diagonally before serving and serve warm.

Nutritional Information per serving:

Calories: 423, Total Fat: 14.2g, Carbs: 9.2g, Protein: 11.3g

CHEESY MIXED VEGETABLE QUESADILLAS

Preparation time: 10 minutes | Cook time: 7 minutes | Servings: 4

Ingredients:

½ small zucchini, grated, drained

½ small red onion, chopped

½ cup frozen corn, defrosted and drained

1 jalapeno pepper seeded and chopped

¼ teaspoon salt

½ (15-ounce) can black beans, drained and rinsed

⅛ teaspoon ground black pepper

½ lb. Monterey Jack cheese, grated

4 (8-inch) tortillas

1 tablespoon vegetable oil

½ teaspoon chili powder

Instructions:

1. Place the zucchini, beans, onion, pepper, corn, jalapenos, salt, and chili powder in a mixing bowl. Toss until well combined.

2. Add the tortillas in a single layer on a 3-inch rack.

3. Divide the vegetable mixture into 4 parts and place each on a tortilla. Sprinkle each with a good amount of cheese.

4. Bake the tortillas on "High" setting at 342° Fahrenheit for about 7 minutes.

5. Take the tortillas out of your oven and fold in half.

6. Slice the quesadillas into halves and serve with your favorite salsa or with a condiment of your choice.

Nutritional Information per serving:

Calories: 382, Total Fat: 12.3g, Carbs: 9.4g, Protein: 6.3g

BACON WRAPPED SHRIMP BITES

Preparation time: 5 minutes | Cook time: 20 minutes | Servings: 2

Ingredients:

6 jumbo shrimp cut in half

⅛ cup sliced water chestnuts

3 slices bacon

Instructions:

1. Chop the bacon into 4 equal parts

2. place a chestnut slice on a shrimp

3. Roll the bacon carefully over the shrimp and chestnut and secure with a toothpick.

4. Place the prepared shrimp rolls on the 3-inch rack and bake on "High" setting at 350° Fahrenheit for 10 minutes per side.

5. Serve hot with a side of your favorite salad.

Nutritional Information per serving:

Calories: 432g, Total Fat: 7.2g, Carbs: 6.3g, Protein: 16.2g

SPICY AND SWEET ROASTED NUTS

Preparation time: 5 minutes | Cook time: 25 minutes | Servings: 2

Ingredients:

1 ½ tablespoons sugar

1 cup pecans

1 cup walnuts

½ large egg white

¼ teaspoon ground cumin

Pinch of cloves

½ teaspoon ground cinnamon

¼ teaspoon salt

½ teaspoon paprika

Instructions:

1. Combine the sugar, salt, paprika, ground cinnamon, ground cloves, and ground cumin. Whisk the egg white until lightly frothy.

2. Add the pecans and walnuts to the whisked egg white and mix well.

3. Pour the prepared spice mix onto the egg white and nuts and toss to coat well.

4. Spread the prepared nut mix in the bottom of the liner pan and cook for about 25 minutes at 350° Fahrenheit.

5. Pause the oven around the 12-minute mark and mix nuts.

6. Rest in the oven until the pan is cool enough to handle. Cool the nuts before serving.

7. Store any leftover nuts in an airtight jar at room temperature, away from direct sunlight. The shelf life of these nuts is 3 days.

Nutritional Information per serving:
Calories: 412, Total Fat: 8.4g, Carbs: 6.4g, Protein: 11.2g

TRIPLE CHEESE GARLIC BREAD

Preparation time: 10 minutes | Cook time: 15 minutes | Servings: 6

Ingredients:

½ loaf Italian bread sliced in half

½ cup mozzarella cheese, shredded

1 tablespoon parmesan cheese

½ cup Asiago cheese, shredded

¼ teaspoon oregano, dried

1 garlic clove, minced

Instructions:

1. Combine garlic, olive oil, and oregano in a bowl.

2. Using the pastry brush, brush the prepared mix onto the cut sides of the bread.

3. In a medium bowl, place the Asiago cheese and top with Parmesan cheese. Add the mozzarella cheese and mix well until combined.

4. Place the garlic and olive oil brushed bread with its cut side up on the 1-inch rack.

5. Top bread with a large amount of cheese and bake on the "High" setting at 350° Fahrenheit for 15 minutes.

6. Let the bread cool slightly and then cut into ½-inch slices.

7. Serve immediately topped with chili flakes and pizza seasoning.

Nutritional Information per serving:
Calories: 389, Total Fat: 12.2g, Carbs: 7.3g, Protein: 12.6g

Chapter 4
Poultry-Based NuWave Oven Recipes

ROASTED DIJON & HERB ENCRUSTED CHICKEN BREAST

Preparation time: 10 minutes | Cook time: 30 minutes | Servings: 2

Ingredients:

2 (5-ounce) chicken breasts, with skin on and bone in

1 tablespoon Dijon mustard

Salt and black pepper to taste

½ teaspoon red pepper flakes

½ teaspoon sugar

1 teaspoon garlic, chopped

2 sprigs parsley leaves, chopped

½ tablespoon olive oil

¼ yellow onion, sliced

Instructions:

1. Combine the Dijon mustard, olive oil, chopped garlic, sugar, red pepper flakes, salt, black pepper, chopped parsley leaves, and sliced yellow onion in a mixing bowl.
2. Add the chicken breasts to the prepared marinade and toss until they are well coated.
3. Place the chicken breasts in an airtight container or a sealable bag and pour the leftover marinade over them.
4. Seal the container or bag and give it a vigorous shake.
5. Refrigerate for at least 4 hours.
6. Place the marinated chicken breasts on a 3-inch rack with skin side down.
7. Bake the chicken breasts for about 15 minutes on "High" setting at 375° Fahrenheit.
8. Flip over and cook for 15 minutes and spoon some leftover marinade over chicken breasts.

9. Once cooked through, let the chicken breasts rest for 5 minutes.

10. Serve hot with some mashed potatoes or a bed of steamed rice.

Nutritional Information per serving:

Calories: 412, Total Fat: 12.3g, Carbs: 9.3g, Protein: 32.g

TURKEY BREAST DISH

Preparation time: 12 minutes | Cook time: 15 minutes | Servings: 2

Ingredients:

2 slices of bacon, thick cut

½ a large head romaine lettuce

2 eggs

⅛ cup olive oil

½ teaspoon Dijon mustard

1 ½ tablespoons red wine vinegar

2 plum tomatoes, diced

½ ripe avocado, pitted, peeled, and diced

1 ½-ounces blue cheese, crumbled

4 ounces roasted turkey breast, cut into cubes

Instructions:

1. Place the eggs on the liner pan on one side of the pan.

2. Place the 4-inch cooking rack on the linear pan. Place the bacon pieces on the side opposite of the eggs.

3. Cook on "High" power at 342° Fahrenheit for about 15 minutes.

4. While the eggs and bacon are cooking arrange the lettuce leaves on top of each other and roll to form a cylinder.

5. Hold the lettuce cylinder tightly and slice into ¼-inch strips.

6. Place the lettuce strips in a large mixing bowl and season to taste.

7. Once the eggs and bacon are done, drain the bacon on a paper towel and remove the cooking rack.

8. Use oven mitts or oven tongs to transfer the eggs to a stream of cold water or place them in an ice bath.

9. Peel the eggs and set aside until cooled.

10. Once the eggs are cooled, chop the drained bacon and eggs into small pieces and set aside.

11. Whisk together the vinegar, oil, pepper, salt, and mustard in a bowl. Whisk until well blended.

12. Add about half of the prepared dressing over the chopped lettuce and toss well until coated. Place the dressing covered lettuce onto a serving dish.

14. Add the diced bacon, turkey, eggs, avocado, blue cheese, and tomatoes over the lettuce, placing each ingredient in one separate section.

15. Season to personal taste with salt and pepper and pour the remaining dressing over the salad and serve immediately.

Nutritional Information per serving:
Calories: 411, Total Fat: 9.3g, Carbs: 7.7g, Protein: 23g

CHICKEN BITES WITH WASABI MAYONNAISE DIPPING SAUCE

Preparation time: 8 minutes | Cook time: 13 minutes | Servings: 2

Ingredients:

1 ½ lbs. chicken breasts, boneless, skinless, cut into ½-inch strips

1 ½ tablespoons olive oil

¼ teaspoon garlic salt

¼ teaspoon black pepper

¼ cup parmesan cheese

1/3 cup white flour

½ teaspoon baking soda

½ egg, slightly beaten

1 teaspoon wasabi

¼ cup mayonnaise

Instructions:

1. Grease a 3-inch cooking rack with cooking spray.

2. In a plastic food storage bag, add the baking soda, garlic salt, flour, cheese, and paprika.

3. Place the chicken strips in the egg until coated and then place the egg coated chicken strips in the bag with the dry flour mix.

4. Seal the bag and shake it until all the chicken pieces are well coated.

5. Place the flour covered chicken strips on the grease 3-inch rack.

6. Lightly sprinkle olive oil over chicken pieces.

7. Bake on "High" setting at 375° Fahrenheit for 13 minutes. At the halfway mark in cook time, flip over the pieces using tongs.

8. Once the chicken is done, allow it to rest for about a minute before serving.

9. Prepare the dipping sauce: combine the mayonnaise and wasabi in a bowl and whisk well.

10. Serve the chicken pieces hot, accompanied with the wasabi mayonnaise dipping sauce.

Nutritional Information per serving:
Calories: 433, Total Fat: 12.4g, Carbs: 8.7g, Protein: 21g

STUFF ROASTED CHICKEN BREAST

Preparation time: 9 minutes | Cook time: 1 hour and 20 minutes | Servings: 1

Ingredients:

1 (8-ounce) chicken breast, boneless

1 cup cooled wild rice

Salt and black pepper to taste

⅛ teaspoon ground cumin

⅛ cup dried golden raisins

⅛ cup green pumpkin seeds

2 cups water

Instructions:

1. Slice a pocket into the chicken breast and set aside.
2. Pour water into a saucepan and heat over a high flame, uncovered until water begins to boil.
3. Place the wild rice into the boiling water and stir well.
4. Reduce the flame to a medium-low and simmer the rice for about an hour.
5. Add the pumpkin seeds, cumin, raisins, salt, and pepper and mix well.
6. Spoon the mixture into the pocket in the chicken breast.
7. Pour olive oil over the stuffed chicken breast.
8. Place the stuffed chicken into a 3-inch cooking rack and roast the chicken for about 20 minutes on each side at 375°Fahrenheit.
9. Heat the juices from the pan until well reduced.
10. Pour the reduced juices over the chicken and serve immediately.

Nutritional Information per serving:
Calories: 462, Total Fat: 12.5g, Carbs: 8.3g, Protein: 24.2g

TURKEY AND APPLE MEATLOAVES

Preparation time: 12 minutes | Cook time: 20 minutes | Servings: 6

Ingredients:

18-ounce turkey mince

2 teaspoons olive oil

2 slices bread, diced

1 onion, finely chopped

1 apple, peeled and grated

1 egg, lightly beaten

Instructions:

1. Grease 6 mini-rectangle oven dishes
2. Mix turkey mince, grated apple, onion, and egg until well combined.
3. Divide the mixture equally among the baking dishes and smooth tops.

4. In a mixing bowl toss diced bread with olive oil. Spread some oiled bread on top of each mini meatloaf.

5. Bake at 350° Fahrenheit in the NuWave Oven on 3-inch rack for 20 minutes.

Nutritional Information per serving:

Calories: 422, Total Fat: 10.3g, Carbs: 9.2g, Protein: 21.2g

CHEESE, CHICKEN & SPINACH PASTA BAKE

Preparation time: 10 minutes | Cook time: 19 minutes | Servings: 4

Ingredients:

- ½ cooked chicken, chopped
- 7 ounces penne pasta or rigatoni
- ½ tablespoon olive oil
- 1 clove garlic
- ¼ cup spinach leaves
- 1 cup pizza cheese blend
- 1 ½ cups of tomato pasta sauce
- ½ red onion, diced
- Salt and pepper to taste

Instructions:

1. Cook your pasta in a saucepan of salted boiling water until just tender. Drain and return to pan.

2. In a pan over medium-high heat, warm your olive oil. Add the garlic with onion to pan and cook for 4 minutes.

3. Add onion mixture, pasta sauce, half of the cheese, and spinach to pasta. Season with salt and pepper, gently tossing to combine.

4. Spoon the pasta mixture into a greased casserole dish. Sprinkle the top with remaining cheese.

5. Bake in your NuWave Oven on 3-inch rack on "High" setting at 342° Fahrenheit for 15 minutes.

Nutritional Information per serving:

Calories: 423, Total Fat: 8.5g, Carbs: 8.2g, Protein: 22.3g

BUFFALO CHICKEN HOAGIE ROLL SANDWICHES

Preparation time: 12 minutes | Cook time: 15 minutes | Servings: 2

Ingredients:

1 ½ tablespoons butter, melted

½ (4-ounce) package blue cheese, crumbled

6 large deli-fried chicken strips

2 tablespoons onion, finely chopped

¾ cup carrots, matchstick cut

¾ cup celery, diagonally sliced

¼ cup Creole seasoning

¼ cup buffalo style hot sauce, divided

2 hoagie rolls

split cup ranch dressing

Instructions:

1. In a mixing bowl, add the butter and about 1 teaspoon of hot sauce together. Whisk with wire whisk.

2. Use a pastry brush to brush the cut sides of the hoagie rolls with the prepared hot sauce butter. In a liner pan, add the hoagie rolls in a single layer with their cut sides up.

3. In another bowl, combine the ranch dressing, creole seasoning, and about 1 teaspoon of hot sauce together.

4. Add in the celery, carrots, and onion to bowl and toss to coat.

5. Place the chicken in the bottom half of the hot sauce/ butter coated rolls.

6. Pour the remaining hot sauce over the rolls.

7. Spoon the celery, carrot, and onion mixture evenly over the chicken and top with cheese. Cover the remaining halves of the rolls.

8. Bake on the "8" setting of your NuWave Oven for about 15 minutes.

9. Serve hot with a side of hot sauce.

Nutritional Information per serving:

Calories: 431, Total Fat: 9.2g, Carbs: 7.3g, Protein: 26.2g

ROASTED CHICKEN IN BBQ SAUCE

Preparation time: 12 minutes | Cook time: 34 minutes | Servings: 4

Ingredients:

½ tablespoon olive oil

1 whole chicken, cut into pieces

¼ cup ketchup

2 garlic cloves, minced

⅛ cup molasses

1 ½ tablespoons Dijon mustard

1/6 cup cider vinegar

¼ cup brown sugar

½ teaspoon hot sauce

Salt and pepper to taste

Instructions:

1. Combine the hot sauce, cider vinegar, brown sugar, molasses, Dijon mustard, garlic cloves, and ketchup in a baking dish.

2. Place the baking dish on the 1-inch cooking rack and cook on "High" setting at 342° Fahrenheit for 10 minutes.

3. Place the chicken pieces in a large mixing bowl. Drizzle the olive oil over the chicken pieces and toss well to coat.

4. Pour some barbeque sauce over the oil coated chicken.

5. Toss until the chicken is well coated in the sauce.

6. Spray cooking spray over the 4-inch cooking rack.

7. Place the barbeque sauce covered chicken pieces on the rack with their skin side down and set on "High" setting at 342° Fahrenheit for 12 minutes.

8. Remove chicken pieces from oven and brush them with the remaining barbeque sauce.

9. Return the chicken pieces to the oven, this time skin side up.

10. Continue cooking on "High" power setting at 342° Fahrenheit for another 12 minutes.

11. Serve hot with a fresh salad on the side.

Nutritional Information per serving:

Calories: 432, Total Fat: 12.4g, Carbs: 7.6g, Protein: 28.2g

THAI CHICKEN WITH ASSORTED VEGETABLES

Preparation time: 8 minutes | Cook time: 20 minutes | Servings: 2

Ingredients:

2 boneless chicken breasts, skinless, boneless

¼ teaspoon red pepper flakes

Pepper and salt to taste

1 teaspoon olive oil

1 cup yellow squash

6 strips red or yellow bell pepper

½ cup zucchini

6 tablespoon Thai sauce

Instructions:

1. Place the chicken breasts on the 1-inch rack.
2. In a mixing bowl, combine Thai sauce and red pepper flakes together.
3. Spoon the prepared sauce over the chicken breasts.
4. Cook the chicken for 10 minutes on "High" setting at 375°Fahrenheit.
5. Place the vegetables in a large sealable bag, add salt and pepper along with olive oil. Seal the bag and toss to coat well.
6. Once the chicken is done, flip it over and spread the remaining sauce over it.
7. Place the oil-coated vegetables around the chicken breasts and continue to cook for an additional 10 minutes. Serve hot.

Nutritional Information per serving:

Calories: 403, Total Fat: 9.6g, Carbs: 6.2g, Protein: 22.3g

GARLIC BBQ CHICKEN

Preparation time: 12 minutes | Cook time: 30 minutes | Servings: 2

Ingredients:

½ whole fryer chicken (1 thigh piece, 1 breast, 1 wing piece, and 1 leg)

1 tablespoon honey mustard

½ tablespoon Worcestershire sauce

1 clove garlic minced

½ tablespoon soy sauce

½ cup BBQ sauce

Instructions:

1. Wash the chicken pieces under running water to clean them. On a 3-inch rack, place the chicken pieces in a single layer.

2. Combine the honey mustard, BBQ sauce, soy sauce, minced garlic, and Worcestershire sauce in a bowl. Whisk using a wire whisk.

3. Brush the prepared sauce over the chicken pieces using a pastry brush, reserving half for the other side.

4. Set your NuWave Oven on the "High" setting at 342° Fahrenheit and grill the chicken for 15 minutes per side.

5. When you flip the chicken pieces over, spoon the remaining prepared sauce over the chicken pieces to keep them moist.

6. Once done, remove the chicken from the oven and let rest for about 5 minutes before serving.

7. Serve hot with a side of grilled vegetables and mashed potatoes.

Nutritional Information per serving:

Calories: 423, Total Fat: 11.3g, Carbs: 8.7g, Protein: 24.2g

HOT & SPICY CHICKEN CURRY

Preparation time: 8 minutes | Cook time: 30 minutes | Servings: 2

Ingredients:

2 teaspoons coriander leaves, chopped

½ cup sour cream

4 tablespoons fresh ginger, grated

2 tablespoons curry powder or paste

4 cloves garlic, minced

2 scallion cut into ½-inch pieces

1 green bell pepper, diced

2 (6-ounce) chicken breasts, cut into bite-size pieces

Salt and black pepper to taste

Instructions:

1. Place the chicken, ginger, salt, scallion, garlic, curry, pepper, and green pepper into a bowl. Toss well to mix.

2. Place the chicken pieces on a 3-inch rack and grill on the "High" setting at 350° Fahrenheit for 15 minutes per side.

3. Remove the chicken pieces from the oven into small baking dish and add in sour cream. Mix well.

4. Place the chicken pieces with the gravy in a serving bowl and serve hot topped with the chopped coriander. Serve with a side of flat bread.

Nutritional Information per serving:
Calories: 412, Total Fat: 8.2g, Carbs: 8.8g, Protein: 23.2g

GRILLED CORNISH GAME HENS WITH POTATOES & ARTICHOKES

Preparation time: 10 minutes | Cook time: 50 minutes | Servings: 2

Ingredients:

1 tablespoon lemon juice

1 tablespoon olive oil

2 cloves garlic

½ teaspoon oregano

1 can artichoke hearts, drained

4-ounces small potatoes, cut into quarters

½ teaspoon thyme

Salt and black pepper to taste

1 (1 ½ lbs.) Cornish game hen, washed and dried with paper towel.

Instructions:

1. Place the lemon juice, olive oil, black pepper, thyme, oregano, salt, garlic, and pepper in a bowl and mix well.

2. Place the drained artichoke hearts and potatoes in mixing bowl. Pour the prepared seasoned oil over the potatoes and artichoke hearts and toss to coat.

3. Use a slotted spoon to drain the excess marinade off the potatoes and artichokes and set aside.

4. Brush the remaining marinade over the game hen and make sure the wing tips of the game hen are twisted under the back.

5. Place the hen on a 1-inch rack. Place the marinated potatoes and artichokes around the marinated hen.

6. Grill on "High" setting at 342° Fahrenheit for 20 minutes per side.

7. Once completely cooked, remove the hen from the oven and allow to rest for 5 minutes before serving.

8. Using a sharp knife cut the hen from the center into two halves.

9. Serve hot with potatoes and artichokes on the side.

Nutritional Information per serving:
Calories: 426, Total Fat: 12.2g, Carbs: 9.2g, Protein: 23.4g

TURKEY BURGERS

Preparation time: 8 minutes | Cook time: 21 minutes | Servings: 2

Ingredients:

½ large shallot, finely chopped

1 tablespoon olive oil

2 hamburger buns or Kaiser rolls

Lettuce leaves

¾ lbs. ground turkey

2 ½ ounces extra sharp cheddar cheese, cut into two slices

Salt and black pepper to taste

Sun Dried Tomato Mayonnaise Ingredients:

⅛ teaspoon salt

⅛ cup mayonnaise

½ tablespoon water

1 teaspoon cider vinegar

⅛ cup oil packed sun-dried tomatoes, drained

Instructions:

1. Place the sun-dried tomatoes, cider vinegar, water, mayonnaise, and salt in a blender and blitz until well blended.

2. Empty the sun-dried tomato mayonnaise in a bowl and cover with a cling wrap. Keep in fridge until burgers are ready.

3. Place the shallots in a baking dish and place it on the 4-inch cooking rack.

4. Cook the shallots on "High" power setting at 342° Fahrenheit for 5 minutes

5. Once done, transfer the shallots to a bowl and season to taste.

6. Add the shallots to the turkey mix and combine.

7. Divide the turkey mix into 4 equal parts and place onto a sheet of wax paper.

8. Pat each quarter until about 1/2 -inch thick.

9. Cover two patties with 1 piece of cheese each.

10. Top the cheese covered patties with leftover patties.

11. Pinch the edges of the two patties to seal the cheese in the middle.

12. Place the prepared stuffed patties onto 4-inch rack and cook for 8 minutes per side.

13. Slice the burger buns and toast the buns on the 4-inch cooking rack for 4 minutes.

14. Place the toasted bun halves on a serving plate, spread the prepared sun-dried tomato mayonnaise on it, place stuffed patties on top, and top with other half of toasted bun.

Nutritional Information per serving:

Calories: 423, Total Fat: 13.2g, Carbs: 8.9g, Protein: 21.1g

CORN, CHICKEN AND CHEESE ENCHILADAS

Preparation time: 10 minutes | Cook time: 25 minutes | Servings: 4

Ingredients:

½ tablespoon olive oil

4 flour tortillas

½ cup grated cheese

¼ cup parsley, fresh chopped

½ cup frozen corn kernels

5.5 ounces of creamed corn

7 ounces chicken, minced

½ teaspoon paprika

½ onion, finely chopped

6.8 ounces jar of tomato & capsicum enchilada sauce

Instructions:

1. Heat the oil in a non-stick pan. Add garlic, onion, and paprika. Cook, stirring occasionally until the onion is soft.

2. Add the chicken to pan, stir until chicken changes color.

3. Add creamed corn and kernels.

4. Bring to boil. Simmer, stirring occasionally, for about 5 minutes or until slightly thickened.

5. Stir in half of the cheese along with parsley.

6. Divide chicken mixture among tortillas and roll up to enclose filling.

7. Spread a third of the sauce over base of a pan about 25cm or an extender pan works well for this. Arrange your tortillas side by side over the sauce. Pour the remaining sauce over top and sprinkle with the remaining cheese.

8. Bake in your NuWave Oven on 3-inch rack; level 10 for 20 minutes. Serve with a garden salad and sour cream.

Nutritional Information per serving:

Calories: 421, Total Fat: 11.2g, Carbs: 8.5g, Protein: 23.2g

CHICKEN, ALMOND & BACON FILLED CROISSANTS

Preparation time: 8 minutes | Cook time: 17 minutes | Servings: 4

Ingredients:

4 croissants

½ cup sour cream

1 tablespoon chives, chopped

2 tablespoons slivered almonds

2 rashers bacon, chopped

¼ chicken, cooked, chopped

Instructions:

1. Toast your almonds in your NuWave Oven on the 3-inch rack at 350° Fahrenheit for 4 minutes.

2. Remove chicken meat from bones and chop finely.

3. Cook bacon in a pan over medium heat for about 5 minutes then drain.

4. Combine the chicken, almonds, chives, bacon, and sour cream.

5. Fill the croissants with the mixture and bake at 350° Fahrenheit in your NuWave Oven on 3-inch rack for 5 minutes.

Nutritional Information per serving:
Calories: 413, Total Fat: 12.4g, Carbs: 9.2g, Protein: 25.2g

GRILLED CILANTRO & GARLIC CHICKEN BREASTS

Preparation time: 9 minutes | Cook time: 30 minutes | Servings: 3

Ingredients:

3 (6-ounce) chicken breasts, skinless and boneless

½ teaspoon black pepper

2 tablespoons lemon or lime juice

½ tablespoon sugar

½ tablespoon soy sauce

½ cup cilantro leaves

2 cloves garlic, peeled

½ small onion, peeled

Instructions:

1. Cover the cutting board with some plastic wrap and tuck the loose ends underneath cutting board.

2. Put the chicken breasts on the plastic wrap covered board and cover with another piece of plastic wrap.

3. Tenderize chicken using a meat tenderizer and flatten to about ½-inch thick.

4. Place the flattened chicken breasts in a large sealable plastic bag.

5. Add onions, cilantro, and garlic in the blender and blitz until finely chopped.

6. Add lemon juice, sugar, soy sauce, and pepper to blender and continue blending until a smooth paste is formed.

7. Pour the prepared sauce into the bag with the chicken breasts, seal it and give the bag a good shake.

8. Place the bag of chicken in the fridge for about 4 hours.

9. Lightly drain the excess marinade from the chicken pieces and place the chicken on the 3-inch rack of your NuWave Oven and grill for 15 minutes per side.

10. Serve the chicken hot with a condiment of your choice.

Nutritional Information per serving:
Calories: 427, Total Fat: 12.3g, Carbs: 9.4g, Protein: 26.2g

CHICKEN PARMESAN

Preparation time: 12 minutes | Cook time: 37 minutes | Servings: 2

Ingredients:

2 (5-ounce) chicken breasts

2 slices provolone cheese

½ (14-ounce) jar marinara sauce

½ tablespoon kosher salt

¼ tablespoon pepper

½ cup flour

2 eggs

½ cup seasoned panko bread crumbs

Instructions:

1. Crack open the eggs in a mixing bowl and season with salt and pepper. Whisk well.

2. Place your flour on another plate and season to taste.

3. In a third shallow plate, add the panko breadcrumbs.

4. Make some light indentations on the chicken breasts using a sharp knife, make sure that you do not slice through.

5. Dip the chicken breasts into the seasoned flour.

6. Dip the flour coated chicken into the eggs.

7. Finally, dip the flour and egg coated chicken into the plate with the breadcrumbs and gently press down to stick crumbs to chicken breasts.

8. Place the chicken breasts on a 3-inch rack and bake on "High" setting at 375° Fahrenheit for 17 minutes per side.

9. Add a piece of provolone on top of each chicken breast and continue baking on "High" setting for another 3 minutes, or until the cheese melts.

10. Place chicken breasts on serving plates and add marinara sauce over them.

Nutritional Information per serving:

Calories: 432, Total Fat: 12.3g, Carbs: 11.5g, Protein: 23.4g

CREAMY CHICKEN BREASTS WITH MUSHROOMS & BELL PEPPERS

Preparation time: 10 minutes | Cook time: 30 minutes | Servings: 2

Ingredients:

2 (6-ounce) chicken breasts

Pepper to taste

Salt to taste

1 cup sour cream

4 large mushrooms, thinly sliced

1 bell pepper, cut into 1-inch pieces

Instructions:

1. Place chicken breasts into an ovenproof dish.

2. Add bell pepper pieces and mushroom slices around chicken breasts.

3. Pour the cream over the chicken and vegetables and spread an even layer on all the ingredients using the back of a spoon. Season to taste with pepper and salt.

4. Place the baking dish on a 3-inch rack and cook on "High" setting at 375°

5. Fahrenheit for about 15 minutes per side.

6. Place the chicken breast on a serving platter and serve hot with a side of sour cream covered bell peppers and mushrooms.

Nutritional Information per serving:

Calories: 435, Total Fat: 12.6g, Carbs: 9.2g, Protein: 24.3g

ROASTED CHICKEN & ONIONS

Preparation time: 9 minutes | Cook time: 20 minutes | Servings: 2

Ingredients:

- 2 chicken breasts, bone in and skin on
- ½ teaspoon sugar
- ½ teaspoon red chili flakes
- ½ teaspoon black pepper
- 1 teaspoon garlic, chopped
- ¼ cup of low sodium chicken stock
- 2 sprigs parsley leaves, chopped
- ¼ yellow onion, sliced
- 1 tablespoon Dijon mustard
- ½ olive oil
- 1 teaspoon salt

Instructions:

1. Combine Dijon mustard, olive oil, parsley leaves, garlic, low sodium chicken stock, sugar, red chili flakes, pepper, and salt in a mixing bowl. Whisk to combine well.

2. Once the mixture is well combined, add the onion and chicken to the bowl.

3. Toss the onion and chicken to totally coat with marinade.

4. Cover mixing bowl with a piece of cling wrap and place in the fridge for 2 hours.

5. Place chicken on the 4-inch cook rack with skin side down.

6. Cook on the "High" setting at 375° Fahrenheit for 10 minutes per side.

7. Allow the chicken to rest once cooked for about five minutes before slicing.

8. Serve chicken over a bed of wild rice or with roasted sweet potatoes.

Nutritional Information per serving:

Calories: 412, Total Fat: 12.4g, Carbs: 9.8g, Protein: 27.2g

CHEESY TURKEY BURGERS

Preparation time: 8 minutes | Cook time: 20 minutes | Servings: 2

Ingredients:

- ½ lb. ground turkey
- 2 whole grain buns
- ½ tablespoon olive oil
- ¼ cup Japanese Panko breadcrumbs
- ½ teaspoon salt
- ½ egg, lightly beaten
- ½ teaspoon black pepper
- 1 scallion or green onion, finely sliced
- ½ lemon, zested and juiced
- ½ garlic clove, finely minced
- 1 (6-ounce) goat cheese log, cut into ½-inch slices

Instructions:

1. Place the turkey, scallions, salt, olive oil, lemon zest, egg, garlic, breadcrumbs, pepper, and lemon juice, in a deep bowl. Mix well until ingredients are incorporated.
3. Divide the turkey mixture into two equal halves.
4. Form each half into a patty about 1-inch thick.
5. Set aside the patties and allow the meat to rest.
6. Slice the buns into two halves and place all 4 pieces onto the 1-inch cooking rack.
7. Cook on "High" setting at 325° Fahrenheit for 6 minutes.
8. Remove the toasted buns from the oven and set aside.
9. Cover the cooking rack with a piece of foil and spray the foil with cooking spray.
10. Place the prepared turkey patties onto the foil.
11. Cook the patties on "High" setting for 8 minutes.
12. Turn the patties over and cook for another 4 minutes.
13. Divide the goat cheese into two equal portions and sprinkle it over the patties.
14. Continue to cook the patties on "High" setting for another 4 minutes.
15. Put the patties on top of the bun bottoms with cheese side facing up.
16. Top with the top of the bun.
17. Serve the burgers hot with a side of French fries.

Nutritional Information per serving:

Calories: 423, Total Fat: 12.5g, Carbs: 10.2g, Protein: 24.3g

Chapter 5
Beef, Lamb & Pork-Based Recipes

CRABMEAT STUFFED BEEF ROULADE

Preparation time: 12 minutes | Cook time: 25 minutes | Servings: 4

Roulade Ingredients:

½ lb. bottom or top round, trimmed beef and butterflied to ½ inch thickness

Pinch of white pepper

¼ lb. fresh spinach, washed and stems removed

Pinch of salt

⅛ cup white wine

⅛ cup parsley, minced

¼ lb. lump crabmeat, with cartilage removed

1 tablespoon olive oil

4-ounces cremini mushrooms, sliced

1 tablespoon butter

Sauce Ingredients:

Pinch of pepper

1 tablespoon unsalted butter

Pinch of salt

½ cup port wine

Instructions for Roulade:

1. Place the butter and the olive oil into a pan and heat it over medium heat for 2 minutes.

2. Add the shallots and onions to the pan and sauté for 5 minutes.

3. Pour the port wine into the pan and cook for 3 minutes or until the wine has evaporated.

4. Add the parsley, crabmeat, and spinach to pan and cook for 5 minutes.

5. Season with salt and pepper to taste. Remove from heat and allow to cool.

6. Place the beef on a flat surface and sprinkle with salt and pepper.

7. Lightly squeeze the crabmeat mixture and remove the extra water from it.

8. Place the crabmeat mixture on the seasoned loin and spread the mixture down the center of the loin, leaving about a half an inch border around the edges.

9. Start rolling the loin over the crabmeat.

10. Tie the roll with kitchen twine at intervals about 1-inch apart.

11. Sprinkle with salt and white pepper on outside of roulade and place the roulade with seam side down on the 4-inch cooking rack.

12. Roast the roulade on "High" setting at 375° Fahrenheit for 6 minutes per side.

13. Remove the roulade from the oven and place it on a cutting board that is loosely covered with a kitchen towel. Allow the roulade to rest for 7 minutes before slicing it.

14. Slice the roulade into 3/4-inch thick slices and serve hot covered in the prepared wine sauce.

Instructions for sauce:

1. In a small pot, pour the port wine and heat it over a high flame until it begins to bubble.

2. Reduce the heat to a simmer and simmer until the wine is reduced to about 1/6 cup.

3. Remove the wine from the heat and add the butter.

4. Whisk the sauce until well blended.

5. Season to taste with salt and pepper and keep warm while the roulade cooks.

Nutritional Information per serving:
Calories: 487, Total Fat: 11.4g, Carbs: 8.9g, Protein: 33.2g

STEAK SANDWICHES

Preparation time: 8 minutes | Cook time: 16 minutes | Servings: 2

Ingredients:

1 (6-ounce) top sirloin steak

2 ½ tablespoons olive oil, divided

½ tablespoon garlic

1 tablespoon parsley

2 French rolls

¼ cup mayonnaise

Salt and black pepper to taste

Instructions:

1. Pour about 1 ½ tablespoons of olive oil over the steak and rub the oil on both sides of steak.

2. Sprinkle steak with salt and pepper on both sides.

3. Place the prepared steak onto the 4-inch cooking rack in your NuWave Oven.

4. Cook on "High" setting for 6 minutes per side.

5. Remove the steak from oven and set aside to cool.

6. Cut the buns open and place them on the 4-inch cooking rack.

7. Toast the buns on "High" setting at 325° Fahrenheit for 4 minutes.

8. While the buns are toasting, mix garlic, mayonnaise, parsley, and remaining olive oil into your blender and blitz until ingredients are emulsified.

9. Once the steak is rested, cut it into ¼ inch slices against the grain.

10. Spread the prepared garlic mayonnaise over the toasted bottom buns and place the steak over them. Cover with the toasted top buns.

11. Serve immediately with a side of French fries or salad.

Nutritional Information per serving:

Calories: 426, Total Fat: 11.6g, Carbs: 12.4g, Protein: 26.3g

STUFFED CABBAGE ROLLS

Preparation time: 12 minutes | Cook time: 25 minutes | Servings: 4

Ingredients:

½ lb. cooked corned beef, chopped

1 egg, lightly beaten

½ cup beef broth

½ head green cabbage; blanched

½ onion, finely chopped

½ cup cooked brown rice

1 ½ celery stalks, finely chopped

Instructions:

1. Put the cooked corned beef and the cooked brown rice together in a mixing bowl. Mix well until well combined.

2. Add the egg, celery, and onion to the mixing bowl. Mix well until well combined.

3. Sprinkle salt and pepper over the beef mixture and mix well.

4. Lay the cabbage leaves on a flat surface and place about 3 tablespoons of beef mixture on each leaf.

5. Roll the leaves up, tucking the sides up as you go.

6. Place the prepared cabbage rolls directly onto the liner pan with the seam down.

7. Pour the beef broth over the rolls.

8. Cover the pan with a piece of aluminum foil and bake at "High" setting at 375°Fahrenheit for 25 minutes.

9. Serve hot with a condiment of your choice.

Nutritional Information per serving:

Calories: 421, Total Fat: 11.8g, Carbs: 11.9g, Protein: 25.3g

THAI STEAK WITH PEANUT SALAD & BEAN SPROUT

Preparation time: 10 minutes | Cook time: 16 minutes | Servings: 4

Marinade Ingredients:

⅛ cup freshly squeezed lime juice

¼ teaspoon red pepper flakes

1 ½ tablespoons vegetable oil

½ tablespoon sugar

⅛ cup rice wine vinegar

½ tablespoon soy sauce

Salad Ingredients:

1 lb. skirt steak

Freshly ground black pepper to taste

½ cup fresh bean sprouts

⅛ cup salted peanuts, chopped

1 small head romaine lettuce, cut crosswise

¼ cup fresh mint leaves

¼ lb. carrots, julienned

Instructions:

1. Pour the lemon juice, rice wine vinegar, soy sauce, and vegetable oil into a blender.
2. Add the sugar and red pepper flakes and blitz until well combined.
3. Sprinkle with salt and pepper over the steak and rub it in using your fingers.
4. Place the seasoned steak into a baking dish.
5. Pour about ¼ of the prepared marinade over the steak, turn steak over to coat all sides.
6. Reserve the remaining marinade.
7. Cover the baking dish and place in the fridge for 4 hours.
8. Remove the steak from the marinade and shake off the excess marinade.
9. Place the steak on the 3-inch cooking rack and cook at 375° Fahrenheit for 8 minutes.
10. Once the steak is cooked transfer the steak to the carving board and allow it to rest for 10 minutes before slicing.
11. While the steak rests, place the carrots, lettuce, sprouts, peanuts, and mint into a large bowl. Pour the reserved marinade over the prepared salad and toss to coat.
13. Slice the steak into slices that are about ¼-inch thick against the grain and then cut the slices into halves in the opposite direction.
14. Spoon the prepared salad onto serving plates and place the steak slices over the bed of salad.

Nutritional Information per serving:

Calories: 423, Total Fat: 11.5g, Carbs: 8.9g, Protein: 26.4g

SHEPARD'S PIE

Preparation time: 10 minutes | Cook time: 44 minutes | Servings: 6

Ingredients:

½ tablespoon olive oil

½ large onion, grated

1 cup parmesan cheese, grated and divided

1 ½ cups mashed potatoes, fresh or leftover

1 egg

½ cup beef stock

2 sprigs thyme, finely chopped

2 sprigs rosemary, finely chopped

3-ounces red wine

1 tablespoon tomato paste

1 tablespoon Worcestershire sauce

1 large carrot, grated

½ lb. ground beef and lamb mix

Salt and black pepper to taste

Instructions:

1. Pour the olive oil into a pot and heat over a high flame until oily is lightly smoking.

2. Add the grated carrot to the pot and sauté for about 3 minutes.

3. Add the onion to pot and mix well. Sauté for 4 minutes.

4. Add the beef and lamb mix to the pot and stir to combine. Continue to cook for 12 minutes or until the meat is browned.

5. If there is too much fat, drain it.

6. Add the tomato paste to the pot and cook for an additional 2 minutes.

7. Add the wine and Worcestershire sauce to pot and stir.

8. Add the beef stock to the pot and continue heating for about 15 minutes until the broth thickens int a thick gravy.

9. Season mixture with salt and pepper to taste and remove pot from heat.

10. Pour the mixture into a large 10-inch baking pan and cover.

11. Place in the fridge for about 1 hour.

12. Add the mashed potatoes to a mixing bowl, with salt and 1 ½ cups of parmesan cheese, egg, and pepper. Mix until well-combined.

13. Spoon the mashed potato mix over the top of the meat mix and smooth using a spoon.

14. Add the remaining cheese on to the top of pie and place it on the 1-inch cooking rack. Bake at 400° Fahrenheit for 17 minutes and serve hot.

Nutritional Information per serving:
Calories: 487, Total Fat: 12.4g, Carbs: 8.5g, Protein: 27.4g

BACON WRAPPED MEATLOAF

Preparation time: 12 minutes | Cook time: 50 minutes | Servings: 6

Ingredients:

21-ounces beef minced

2 cloves garlic, minced

1 cup breadcrumbs

½ cup spaghetti sauce

1 tablespoon dry Italian herbs

2 large eggs

¼ cup parmesan cheese, grated

7-ounces bacon rashers, thinly sliced

Piece of baking paper a bit larger than a bread loaf pan

Instructions:

1. Spray loaf pan with the oil and line pan with bacon rashers leaving extra length hanging over the sides of the pan.

2. Mix together the remaining ingredients.

3. Fill loaf pan with meat mixture and bring the ends of bacon rashers into centre to seal.

4. Bake in your NuWave Oven on 3-inch rack on level 10 for 20 minutes.

5. Carefully turn meatloaf over onto baking paper (on rack) and remove the loaf pan. Cook for an additional 30 minutes.

BACON, LIVER & ONIONS

Preparation time: 8 minutes | Cook time: 25 minutes | Servings: 2

Ingredients:

½ lb. calf liver, ½-inch thick

4 slices bacon, cut in half

1 medium onion, sliced into rings

Salt and black pepper to taste

¼ cup milk

Instructions:

1. Put the liver into a mixing bowl.

2. Add the milk, pepper, and salt into bowl and mix well.

3. Cover and allow to rest for an hour.

4. Place the onion rings on a 3-inch cooking rack

5. Drain the liver from the marinade and shake excess marinade off. Place the liver on the onion slices.

6. Place the bacon slices on the liver.

7. Cook for about 8 minutes at 350° Fahrenheit.

8. Remove the bacon slices from the liver and flip the liver over. Return the bacon slices to the liver. Continue to cook for an additional 10 minutes.

9. Once cooked, allow the liver to rest in oven (with dome on) for another 7 minutes.

10. Serve hot with bacon and onions.

Nutritional Information per serving:

Calories: 422, Total Fat: 10.2g, Carbs: 6.3g, Protein: 28.6g

RIB ROAST

Preparation time: 5 minutes | Cook time: 48 minutes | Servings: 2

Ingredients:

½ teaspoon onion powder

1 (2 ½ lb.) standing rib roast, thawed

Salt and black pepper to taste

Instructions:

1. Combine salt, onion powder, and black pepper in a small bowl.

2. Place the rib roast on a cutting board.

3. Sprinkle the rub over the rib roast and rub it in using your fingers.

4. Place the rib roast on the 1-inch rack with rib side down.

5. Grill on "High" setting at 400°Fahrenheit for 16 minutes per pound of ribs.

6. Remove the ribs from the oven and allow them to rest for 10 minutes before slicing them.

7. Serve hot with barbeque sauce on the side.

Nutritional Information per serving:

Calories: 487, Total Fat: 12.4g, Carbs: 7.6g, Protein: 28.7g

JACK O' PEPPERS

Preparation time: 10 minutes | Cooking time: 30 minutes | Servings: 3

Ingredients:

3 bell peppers

1 tablespoon garlic, minced

½ onion, diced

¼ cup mushrooms, diced

1 cup wild rice, cooked

¼ lb. ground beef

⅛ cup Italian sausage

Instructions:

1. Use a sharp knife to carve a jack o' lantern face in the peppers. Slice the top of the peppers and reserve the tops for later.
2. Add the beef, wild rice, mushrooms, garlic, salt, pepper, and Italian sausage into a large mixing bowl. Mix well.
3. Spoon the stuffing into carved peppers, until the jack o' lantern face is filled.
4. Place the peppers on 3-inch cooking rack.
5. Bake for 20 minutes at 350° Fahrenheit.
6. Once the cook time is completed, place the reserve tops on top of peppers.
7. Continue to bake at 350° Fahrenheit for another 10 minutes.
8. Transfer peppers to serving dishes and serve hot.

Nutritional Information per serving:
Calories: 432, Total Fat: 9.2g, Carbs: 6.3g, Protein: 25.2g

VEGGIE & STEAK TORTILLA ROLLS

Preparation time: 8 minutes | Cook time: 17 minutes | Servings: 6

Ingredients:

15-ounces flank steak

½ green pepper

1 medium Spanish onion

½ red pepper

½ package fajita or taco seasoning mix

½ yellow pepper

4-ounces ready made salsa

4-ounces cheddar cheese, shredded

6 ready-made tortillas

Salt and black pepper to taste

Instructions:

1. Slice the steak into thin strips. Chop up the Spanish onion, and the red, yellow, and green peppers.

2. Sprinkle the taco mix on the steak strips and toss until well coated.

3. Arrange the vegetables on the outside of a 3-inch rack and place steak strips on the inside.

4. Cook on the "High" setting at 400°Fahrenheit for 17 minutes, about 8-9 minutes per side.

5. Place the tortillas in a piece of foil and seal foil shut.

6. Place the foil wrapped tortillas in the liner pan when you open the dome to flip the steak and vegetables over.

7. Once the steak is done cooking, remove it and the vegetables from the oven.

8. Carefully unwrap the tortillas from the foil.

9. Place the grilled vegetables in a single layer over the warmed tortillas.

10. Layer the steak strips over the vegetables.

11. Sprinkle some cheese over the steak and top with salsa.

12. Roll the tortillas lightly and serve hot with a salad on the side.

Nutritional Information per serving:

Calories: 463, Total Fat: 11.2g, Carbs: 9.3g, Protein: 27.2g

SOUR & SWEET LAMB CHOPS

Preparation time: 10 minutes | Cook time: 8 minutes | Servings: 2

Ingredients:

½ tablespoon red wine vinegar

2 (1-inch thick) lamb chops

1/4 teaspoon garlic powder

½ teaspoon dark brown sugar

¼ teaspoon ground sage

¼ teaspoon pepper

Instructions:

1. Whisk together the red wine vinegar, ground sage, garlic powder, brown sugar, and pepper in a bowl.

2. Pour the prepared spice rub over the lamb chops and rub the seasoning into the meat using your fingers. Place the lamb chops on the 4-inch cooking rack.

3. Cook on "High" power setting at 375°Fahrenheit for about 8 minutes for medium cooked lamb chops.

4. Serve hot with a side of mashed potatoes or roasted vegetables.

Nutritional Information per serving:

Calories: 427, Total Fat: 11.2g, Carbs: 8.6g, Protein: 25.3g

TARRAGON AND BUTTER STUFFED LAMB CHOPS

Preparation time: 8 minutes | Cook time: 14 minutes | Servings: 3

Ingredients:

3 (2-inch) lamb chops

½ tablespoon tarragon, fresh chopped

½ large shallot, chopped

½ tablespoon parsley, fresh chopped

½ stick soft, un-salted butter

2 cloves garlic, minced

Instructions:

1. Place the softened butter into a mixing bowl.

2. Add the parsley, shallot, tarragon, garlic, salt, and pepper. Mix well until the ingredients are well combined.

3. Spoon mixture into lamb pockets and hold them in place using toothpicks.

4. Arrange the lamb chops in a single layer on the 3-inch cooking rack.

5. Cook on "High" setting at 400°Fahrenheit for about 7 minutes per side for medium rare done lamb chops and serve hot.

Nutritional Information per serving:

Calories: 467, Total Fat: 10.2g, Carbs: 9.2g, Protein: 26.4g

ROSEMARY, THYME CRUSTED LAMB SHANKS

Preparation time: 10 minutes | Cook time: 16 minutes | Servings: 3

Ingredients:

3 lamb shanks

1 ½ tablespoons white wine

½ (14-ounce) can crushed tomatoes

¾ cup vegetables stock

½ tablespoon Worcestershire sauce

1 bay leaf

1 tablespoon thyme, fresh

½ sprig rosemary, fresh

½ red onion, chopped

1 clove garlic, crushed

Salt and pepper to taste

Instructions:

1. Arrange the lamb shanks in a single layer on the 4-inch cooking rack.
2. Cook on "High" setting at 375°Fahrenheit for 8 minutes per side.
3. Place the roasted lamb shanks in a mixing bowl.
4. Combine the garlic, onion, rosemary, thyme, bay leaf, Worcestershire sauce, vegetable stock, crushed tomatoes, white wine, pepper, and salt in a small mixing bowl.
5. Pour the prepared marinade over the lamb shanks and toss well to coat.
6. Place the lamb shanks with marinade in the liner pan.
7. Cook on the level 7 power setting for 4 hours.
8. Make sure to pause the oven at regular intervals to turn the shanks over to ensure even cooking.
9. Serve hot over a bed of mashed potatoes.

Nutritional Information per serving:

Calories: 432, Total Fat: 10.2g, Carbs: 9.2g, Protein: 27.3g

LAMB BURGERS WITH ORANGE & OLIVE SALSA

Preparation time: 10 minutes | Cook time: 20 minutes | Servings: 8

Ingredients:

- 2 ⅔ lbs. ground lamb
- 8 burger buns of your choice
- 1 teaspoon paprika
- 2 teaspoons salt
- 2 large shallots
- 1 ½ teaspoons ground black pepper
- 4 tablespoons cilantro, fresh, chopped
- 2 cloves garlic, minced
- 2 jalapenos, seeded and minced

Salsa Ingredients:

- ½ cup green olives, chopped and pitted
- 4 large oranges, peel and remove pith, cut into 1/3-inch cubes
- 2 cups chopped red onion
- 2 tablespoons lemon juice, fresh
- 2 tablespoons honey
- 4 tablespoons olive oil

Instructions:

1. Place the ground lamb in a mixing bowl.
2. Add in the jalapenos, garlic, cilantro, ground black pepper, salt, cumin, paprika, and shallots.
3. Mix until all the ingredients are well combined.
4. Divide the lamb mixture into 8 equal parts and flatten to make 1-inch patties.
5. Grease 3-inch cooking rack with some butter or cooking spray.
6. Arrange the prepared burger patties in a single layer on the greased 3-inch cooking rack.
7. Cook on "High" power setting at 380°Fahrenheit for 10 minutes per side.

8. In another mixing bowl, combine fresh lemon juice, olive oil, honey, red onion, orange cubes, and green olives.

9. Place the lamb patties on the burger buns and spoon the prepared salsa over them and serve hot.

Nutritional Information per serving:
Calories: 443, Total Fat: 11.3g, Carbs: 7.6g, Protein: 27.3g

HERB BUTTER STUFFED LAMB CHOPS

Preparation time: 12 minutes | Cook time: 24 minutes | Servings: 3

Ingredients:

3 (2-inch) lamb chops

½ tablespoon tarragon, fresh chopped

½ large shallot, chopped

½ tablespoon parsley, fresh chopped

½ stick butter, unsalted and soft

2 cloves garlic, minced

½ teaspoon salt

¼ teaspoon ground black pepper

Instructions:

1. Place the parsley, shallots, garlic, pepper, and salt in a mixing bowl. Mix well.

2. Add the butter and whisk until well combined.

3. Place the lamb chops on a cutting board covered in plastic wrap. Cover with another piece of plastic wrap and lightly hammer the lamb chops with a meat tenderizer until they are flattened (about ½-inch thick).

4. Spoon equal amounts of your prepared herb butter onto your lamb chops.

5. Roll your lamb chops and secure them with some toothpicks.

6. Place your stuffed lamb chops into your NuWave Oven on the 3-inch cooking rack.

7. Grill the lamb chops on the "High" setting at 400°Fahrenheit for 12 minutes per side.

8. When lamb chops are cooked, remove them from oven and allow them to rest for 5 minutes before serving.

9. Serve the lamb chops hot with a side of hot sauce.

Nutritional Information per serving:
Calories: 456, Total Fat: 12.2g, Carbs: 8.5g, Protein: 26.3g

MUSTARD & THYME CRUSTED LAMB

Preparation time: 10 minutes | Cook time: 40 minutes | Servings: 4

Ingredients:

1 medium boneless leg of lamb (about 2 lbs.)

1 tablespoon rosemary, chopped

2 cloves garlic, finely chopped

1 tablespoon thyme, chopped

2 tablespoons Dijon mustard

1 tablespoon salt

1 teaspoon fresh ground pepper

For Sauce:

1 tablespoon sugar, adjust per taste

¼ teaspoon ground pepper

½ tablespoon salt

½ cup mint, chopped fresh

1 tablespoon olive oil

2 tablespoons white wine vinegar

Instructions:

1. Place the lamb on a clean, dry, flat working surface. Use a sharp knife to trim off the extra fat from the lamb. Make some deep cuts in the thicker parts of the lamb.

2. Cover the lamb with a piece of plastic and use a meat tenderizer to flatten the lamb until it is uniformly thick.

3. Sprinkle a generous amount of salt and pepper on both sides of lamb.

4. Combine the thyme, salt, garlic, mustard, rosemary, and pepper together in a small mixing bowl.

5. Spread the spice rub over the lamb and place the lamb into a safe baking dish.

6. Cover the baking dish and place in the fridge for 2 hours.

7. Roll the lamb into a thick roll and fasten it in place using some kitchen twine.

8. Roast on the "High" power setting at 375°Fahrenheit for 20 minutes per pound of meat for medium doneness.

9. Flip the meat over around halfway mark.

10. While your lamb is roasting, prepare the mint sauce.

11. Pour about 2 tablespoons of water in a mixing bowl. Add the salt, sugar, and pepper and whisk.

12. Add in the mint, oil, and vinegar and continue whisking until smooth.

13. Taste and adjust the sugar, salt, and pepper to taste.

14. When the lamb is done cooking, allow it to rest for 12 minutes before slicing.

15. Serve hot with the prepared mint sauce on the side.

Nutritional Information per serving:
Calories: 453, Total Fat: 12.3g, Carbs: 8.9g, Protein: 26.7g

FETA & TOMATO TOPPED GRILLED LAMB CHOPS

Preparation time: 12 minutes | Cook time: 17 minutes | Servings: 2

Ingredients:

2 (1-inch) lamb chops

½ clove garlic

½ tablespoon lemon juice

1 tablespoon olive oil

2 tablespoons chopped ripe tomatoes

3 Kalamata olives, pitted

Salt and pepper to taste

½ tablespoon parsley, chopped

2-ounces feta cheese, crumbled

Instructions:

1. Combine the lemon juice, olive oil, and garlic together in a shallow dish.

2. Place the lamb chops in the marinade and turn the lamb chops over until they are well coated.

3. Cover the dish with a piece of plastic wrap and place in the fridge for 30 minutes.

4. In a small mixing bowl, combine olives, tomato, feta, and parsley and set aside.

5. Place the marinated lamb chops on the 3-inch rack in your NuWave Oven. Season with salt and pepper.

6. Grill the lamb chops on "High" setting at 400°Fahrenheit for 12 minutes, flipping over halfway through cook time.

7. When the cook time is completed, divide the feta mix evenly between the lamb chops.

8. Top each lamb chop with a portion of the prepared feta cheese mix.

9. Grill on "High" setting at 400°Fahrenheit for 5 minutes or until the cheese melts.

10. Serve hot with a side of your favorite side dish.

Nutritional Information per serving:

Calories: 467, Total Fat: 12.4g, Carbs: 9.2g, Protein: 27.3g

MUSTARD COATED LEG OF LAMB

Preparation time: 8 minutes | Cook time: 60 minutes | Servings: 4

Ingredients:

1 (1 ½ lbs.) boneless leg of lamb, fat trimmed

2 large carrots, diced

2 tablespoons pistachios, roasted and salted

1 ½ tablespoons olive oil, divided

2 parsley roots, leaves removed and roots cut in half lengthwise

½ celery root, diced

4 baby Yukon gold potatoes, cut in half

½ turnip, large, diced

Salt and black pepper to taste

4 garlic cloves, roughly chopped

½-ounce rosemary, minced

1 tablespoon Dijon mustard

1 tablespoon thyme, minced

Instructions:

1. Place the Yukon potatoes, parsley roots, carrots, and celery root into a mixing bowl.

2. Add in the olive oil, black pepper, salt, and thyme. Toss well until all vegetables are coated.

3. Add in the pistachios and transfer the mixture into the liner pan.

4. Put the leg of lamb onto a flat, dry work surface.

5. Score the surface of the leg of lamb with a sharp knife.

6. Spread the mustard on the fat side of the leg.

7. Sprinkle the rosemary, garlic, black pepper, and salt over leg of lamb.

8. Place the seasoned lamb over the vegetables in the liner pan.

9. Cook on "High" setting at 380°Fahrenheit for an hour or until food is well browned and tender. Serve hot.

Nutritional Information per serving:

Calories: 464, Total Fat: 11.2g, Carbs: 8.4g, Protein: 28.2g

BARBEQUE LAMB SKEWERS

Preparation time: 10 minutes | Cook time: 25 minutes | Servings: 2

Ingredients:

1 lb. leg of lamb, fat trimmed, cut into 2-inch cubes

2 Roma tomatoes, cut in half and seeded

Barbeque sauce

4 large white mushrooms

½ large green bell pepper, cored and sliced into 4 equal pieces

½ red onion, quartered

Instructions:

1. Divide the lamb cubes, onion quarters, and green pepper pieces into two equal portions.

2. Thread the lamb cubes, green pepper slices, mushrooms, Roma tomatoes, and onion quarters onto bamboo or metal skewers in an alternating pattern of meat and vegetables.

3. Place the prepared skewers on the 3-inch rack and lightly brush the barbeque sauce over them.

4. Grill the skewers at "High" setting at 400°Fahrenheit for 15 minutes.

5. Flip the skewers and again brush them with the barbeque sauce.

6. Grill for another 10 minutes. Serve hot with some barbeque sauce on the side.

Nutritional Information per serving:
Calories: 425, Total Fat: 8.7g, Carbs: 7.2g, Protein: 24.5g

ROSEMARY & LAMB COTTAGE PIE

Preparation time: 12 minutes | Cook time: 45 minutes | Servings: 4

Ingredients:

28-ounces potatoes, peeled and chopped

1 ½ cups beef stock

2 tablespoons plain flour

1 teaspoon rosemary, dried

2 tablespoons tomato paste

2 carrots, grated

17.5-ounces lamb mince

2 cloves garlic, chopped

1 onion, finely diced

1 tablespoon olive oil

¼ cup milk

1 tablespoon butter

½ cup cheese, grated

Instructions:

1. Place the potatoes in a pan of boiling water that is salted for 20 minutes, then drain. Add milk and butter and mash until smooth.

2. Heat the oil in a pan over medium heat. Add garlic and onions and cook for 5 minutes.

3. Add the tomato paste and rosemary, cook stirring for 2 minutes. Remove from heat.

4. Stir in the flour and slowly add the beef stock and stir until well combined. Return to heat and cook for an additional 5 minutes. Spoon into 23cm pie dish.

5. Top with mashed potatoes and sprinkle top with cheese.

6. Bake in NuWave Oven on 3-inch rack for 15 minutes at 350°Fahrenheit or until golden.

Nutritional Information per serving:
Calories: 467, Total Fat: 12.3g, Carbs: 8.9g, Protein: 27.3g

SAUSAGES WITH BACON & PRUNES

Preparation time: 8 minutes | Cook time: 15 minutes | Servings: 2

Ingredients:

4 thick sausages

2 rashers bacon

12 prunes, pitted

Instructions:

1. Using a sharp knife, gently make a slit in each sausage without cutting right through. Into each sausage, stuff 3 prunes into slit.

2. Cut each of the bacon rashers into 2 lengthways and diagonally wrap around sausage and fix with a cocktail stick.

3. Bake in NuWave Oven on the 3-inch cooking rack, level 10 for 15 minutes, turning sausages after 10 minutes.

Nutritional Information per serving:
Calories: 432, Total Fat: 9.2g, Carbs: 7.3g, Protein: 22.1g

BACON OMELETS

Preparation time: 10 minutes | Cook time: 15 minutes | Servings: 3

Ingredients:

- ½ tablespoon parsley
- ¼ cup green pepper, chopped
- ⅛ cup onion, chopped
- ½ cup beef bacon, chopped into bite sized pieces
- ¼ cup milk
- 3-ounces cheddar cheese, shredded
- 5 eggs

Instructions:

1. Put the eggs into a mixing bowl, add milk and whisk until eggs are fluffy in texture.
2. Add in the cheese, bacon, green pepper, and onion and mix well.
3. Pour the egg and bacon mixture into a 4-inch by 4-inch silicon baking dish.
4. Place the dish onto the 1-inch cooking rack. Set to "High" setting at 350° Fahrenheit and bake for 15 minutes.
5. Allow the eggs to sit in the dome for another minute with the heat off.
6. Extract the egg from the silicon-baking dish and cut into pieces.
7. Serve hot with a side of baked English muffins or whole wheat bread.

Nutritional Information per serving:
Calories: 372, Total Fat: 9.3g, Carbs: 7.3g, Protein: 20.1g

HOT & SPICY CLAMS & SAUSAGE

Preparation time: 9 minutes | Cook time: 15 minutes | Servings: 1

Ingredients:

- 16 littleneck clams, cleaned
- 2 sausages, crumbled
- 2 cloves garlic, minced

Hot sauce to taste

Lemon slices as needed

Cilantro, fresh chopped to taste

Instructions:

1. Put the sausage and clams in a mixing bowl together.

2. Add in the garlic, cilantro, and hot sauce and toss until well coated.

3. Arrange the clam and sausage mix in the bottom of liner pan.

4. Cook on "High" setting at 350°Fahrenheit for 15 minutes.

5. Serve hot topped with lemon slices.

Nutritional Information per serving:

Calories: 362, Total Fat: 7.2g, Carbs: 6.4g, Protein: 21.3g

APPLE TARTINES WITH HAM & BRIE

Preparation time: 10 minutes | Cook time: 18 minutes | Servings: 8

Ingredients:

2 apples, thinly sliced

4 slices French bread

6-ounces Brie cheese

¼ lbs. ham, thinly sliced

Instructions:

1. Place the bread slices on a cookie sheet and place them into Nuwave Oven to brown the edges set at 450°Fahrenheit for 8 minutes.

2. Remove them and place the slices of apples, ham, and Brie on top of them.

3 Put the tartines back into NuWave Oven for 10 minutes.

4. Remove from the oven and cut each slice of bread into four pieces.

Nutritional Information per serving:

Calories: 402, Total Fat: 8.5g, Carbs: 7.5g, Protein: 20.2g

SAUSAGES WITH MAPLE SAUCE & FIGS

Preparation time: 8 minutes | Cook time: 22 minutes | Servings: 4

Ingredients:

2 tablespoons balsamic vinegar, divided

8 sausages

2 tablespoons olive oil

2 tablespoons maple syrup

8 figs, ripe

1 ½ lbs. Swiss chard

½ sweet onion, large

Salt and pepper to taste

Instructions:

1. Mix 1 tablespoon of balsamic vinegar and maple syrup in a small mixing bowl. Place the sausages and figs on a foil-lined NuWave Oven tray, and brush with mixture.

2. Roast for 10 minutes at 450° Fahrenheit or until golden. Brushing the remaining mixture on during half time.

3. Microwave the onion on high power for 9 minutes, add oil, salt, pepper, and remaining vinegar and heat for an additional 3 minutes.

4. Serve with Swiss chard.

BACON CORN MUFFINS

Preparation time: 10 minutes | Cook time: 17 minutes | Servings: 6

Ingredients:

1 ¼ cup of self-rising cornmeal mix

¼ cup butter, melted

¾ cup buttermilk

1 cup cooked bacon, chopped

Instructions:

1. Mix the bacon, cornmeal mix, egg, buttermilk, and butter in a mixing bowl.

2. Pour this batter into a muffin pan that has been lightly greased or sprayed with cooking spray. Fill ¾ of the muffin cups.

3. Bake for 17 minutes at 425°Fahrenheit in your NuWave Oven.

4. Cool on wire rack for 10 minutes.

Nutritional Information per serving:

Calories: 327, Total Fat: 5.2g, Carbs: 6.5g, Protein: 23.2g

MOROCCAN PORK KEBABS

Preparation time: 10 minutes | Cook time: 45 minutes | Servings: 4

Ingredients:

1 ½-ounces pork loin, boneless

1 red onion

1 eggplant

1 half-pint tzatziki

Pita bread

2 tablespoons mint, chopped

½ cucumber, sliced

¼ cup orange juice

1 garlic clove, chopped

4 tablespoons olive oil

1 ½ teaspoons salt

¾ teaspoon pepper

⅛ tablespoon ground cumin

Instructions:

1. Put the oil, salt, pepper, cumin, tomato paste, cinnamon, orange juice, garlic, and pork into a mixing bowl.

2. Add the salt, pepper, and oil to the onion and eggplant. Skewer them.

3. Bake them in your NuWave Oven for 20 minutes at 425° Fahrenheit.

4. Skewer the pork too. Add to a baking tray and bake for 20 minutes.

5. Put the bread over the pork and bake for another 5 minutes.

6. Add tzatziki, mint, and cucumber on the side and serve the dish.

Nutritional Information per serving:

Calories: 432, Total Fat: 11.3g, Carbs: 7.6g, Protein: 25.4g

ASIAN STYLE PORK CHOPS WITH A TANGY PINEAPPLE RELISH

Preparation time: 10 minutes | Cook time: 24 minutes | Servings: 2

Ingredients:

2 (1-1 ½-inch thick) pork chops

¼ teaspoon black pepper

½ teaspoon ground ginger

2 tablespoons soy sauce

2 cloves garlic, chopped

2 tablespoons extra virgin olive oil

½ tablespoon brown sugar

2 tablespoons red onion, sliced

½ cup fresh or canned pineapple

Salt and pepper to taste

1 ½ tablespoons flat leaf parsley, chopped

Instructions:

1. Place the ginger, soy sauce, brown sugar, oil, and pepper together in a sealable freezer bag. Shake well until combined.

2. Place the pork chops into the bag with the marinade. Place in the fridge for 4 hours.

3. Add the pork chops onto the 3-inch cooking rack and cook at "High" setting at 342° Fahrenheit for 12 minutes per side.

4. While the pork chops are cooking, place the pineapple, parsley, pepper, salt, and onion in a medium-bowl. Mix well until just combined to make the pineapple relish.

5. When the pork is cooked, remove it from the oven and allow it to rest for 5 minutes before slicing.

6. Serve hot topped with pineapple relish and with salad on the side.

Nutritional Information per serving:

Calories: 446, Total Fat: 11.2g, Carbs: 8.4g, Protein: 26.5g

THAI STYLE GRILLED PORK TENDERLOIN

Preparation time: 12 minutes | Cook time: 40 minutes | Servings: 3

Ingredients:

1 (12-ounce) pork tenderloin

1 tablespoon sweet Asian chili sauce

½ tablespoon soy sauce

1 ½ tablespoons hoisin sauce

1 tablespoon lime or lemon juice

1 tablespoon fresh cilantro, chopped

½ tablespoon ginger root, chopped

½ tablespoon sesame oil

Instructions:

1. Place the ginger root, garlic, lemon or lime juice, fresh cilantro, hoisin sauce, soy sauce, sweet Asian chili sauce, and sesame oil in a mixing bowl. Whisk well using a wire whisk until well combined.

2. Place the pork tenderloin in a baking dish just large enough to hold the pork tenderloin.

3. Pour the prepared sauce over the tenderloin and turn the tenderloin around a few times to coat.

4. Cover the baking dish with a cling wrap and place in the fridge for 6 hours.

5. Lightly shake the excess marinade off the pork tenderloin and place it on the 3-inch rack. Grill on "High" setting for 350°Fahrenheit for 20 minutes per side.

6. Once the meat is cooked to perfection, remove it from the oven and let it rest for 5 minutes before slicing it. Cut the tenderloin diagonally.

7. Serve hot with a side of roasted potatoes or vegetables.

Nutritional Information per serving:
Calories: 453, Total Fat: 11.7g, Carbs: 9.2g, Protein: 27.3g

CASSEROLE WITH SAUSAGE, RICE & VEGETABLES

Preparation time: 12 minutes | Cook time: 40 minutes | Servings: 3

Ingredients:

½ (10 ½ -ounce) can condensed cream of celery soup, undiluted

½ cup cheddar cheese, grated

½ lb. sausage, sliced into ½-inch pieces

½ (10-ounce) package of frozen peas, thawed

¾ cup instant rice

½ cup water

½ tablespoon butter

½ (10-ounce) package frozen corn, thawed

Instructions:

1. Pour the cream of celery soup into a pan.
2. Add butter and water and mix well.
3. Heat the pan over a high flame and mix, cooking for 5-minutes.
4. Add in the rice and take the pan off heat. Cover and let the rice stand for 7 minutes.
5. Add in the peas, corn, and sausage into pan and mix well.
6. Pour the mixture into an ovenproof baking dish and place in the liner pan.
7. Set the oven to "High" setting at 375°Fahrenheit and bake for 25 minutes.
8. Sprinkle with cheese and bake for another 3 minutes. Serve hot.

Nutritional Information per serving:
Calories: 423, Total Fat: 11.2g, Carbs: 9.2g, Protein: 25.3g

Chapter 6
Vegetable-Based NuWave Oven Recipes

RICOTTA & SPINACH STUFFER LASAGNA ROLLS

Preparation time: 12 minutes | Cook time: 40 minutes | Servings: 3

Ingredients:

4 lasagna noodles, cooked, drained

2 tablespoons mushrooms, chopped

¼ teaspoon thyme leaves

½ cup tomato sauce

½ tablespoon butter

½ medium onion, finely chopped

1 clove garlic, minced

¼ teaspoon basil, dried

1 (5-ounce) package frozen chopped spinach

1 tablespoon parmesan cheese

½ cup Ricotta or cottage cheese

Black pepper to taste

¼ teaspoon oregano, dried

Instructions:

1. Heat the butter in a pan with the garlic and onion for 3 minutes.

2. Add the tomato sauce and mix well.

3. Add the thyme, oregano, and basil and cook for 1 minute. Add in the mushrooms and let the sauce simmer for 10 minutes. Remove the sauce from heat and set it aside.

4. Follow instruction on spinach package to cook spinach. Drain spinach and squeeze out any excess water. Place the spinach, pepper, Ricotta (or cottage cheese), and parmesan cheese in a blender. Blitz until smooth. Spoon the mixture onto the end of lasagna noodle.

5. Roll the noodle tightly to contain the filling in. Repeat with the rest of noodles. Place the noodle rolls into a liner pan that has been sprayed with cooking spray. Pour the prepared sauce over noodle rolls. Cook on "High" setting at 342°Fahrenheit for about 25 minutes. Serve hot.

Nutritional Information per serving:

Calories: 354, Total Fat: 4.7g, Carbs: 5.6g, Protein: 6.4g

ROASTED BUTTERNUT SQUASH

Preparation time: 8 minutes

Cooking time: 45 minutes | Servings: 2

Ingredients:

Olive oil as needed

1 teaspoon sugar

1 teaspoon salt

½ butternut squash, cut in half lengthwise and seeds removed

Instructions:

1. Prepare the squash. Pour the olive oil over the squash.

2. Combine the sugar and salt and rub it over the butternut squash half.

3. Place the butternut squash half on a 1-inch rack.

4. Cook on "High" setting at 350°Fahrenheit for 45 minutes.

5. Chop the roasted squash into cubes.

6. Transfer the roasted squash cubes onto a serving plate.

7. Serve hot, topped with some olive oil for garnish.

Nutritional Information per serving:

Calories: 343, Total Fat: 4.2g, Carbs: 6.2g, Protein: 5.4g

ROASTED CAULIFLOWER, OLIVES & CHICKPEAS

Preparation time: 10 minutes | Cook time: 24 minutes | Servings: 3

Ingredients:

- 3 cups cauliflower florets
- ¼ teaspoon salt
- 1 ½ tablespoons fresh flat leaf parsley
- ¼ teaspoon crushed red pepper flakes
- ½ (15-ounce) can chickpeas, rinsed and drained
- ½ cup Spanish green olives, pitted
- 4 cloves garlic, chopped

Instructions:

1. Place the cauliflower florets, olives, garlic, chickpeas, crushed red pepper, and salt into a mixing bowl.
2. Pour the olive oil over the ingredients and allow to stand for 3 minutes.
3. Toss until all the ingredients are well coated.
4. Place the olive oil coated ingredients in the bottom of a liner pan in a single layer.
5. Cook on "High" setting at 325°Fahrenheit for 24 minutes.
6. Serve hot with your preferred condiment on the side.

Nutritional Information per serving:

Calories: 346, Total Fat: 4.5g, Carbs: 5.6g, Protein: 4.7g

ROASTED GARLIC MUSHROOMS

Preparation time: 8 minutes | Cook time: 25 minutes | Servings: 2

Ingredients:

- 1 (8-ounce) package button mushrooms, quartered
- 2 cloves garlic, finely chopped
- 2 tablespoons olive oil
- 1 tablespoon fresh thyme, chopped

Instructions:

1. Place the oil, fresh thyme, and garlic in a small mixing bowl.
2. Season to taste with salt and pepper.
3. Pour the marinade over the mushrooms and toss until the mushrooms are well coated.
4. Place the marinated mushrooms directly onto the liner pan.
5. Roast on the "High" setting at 325°Fahrenheit for 25 minutes. Serve hot.

Nutritional Information per serving:
Calories: 328, Total Fat: 4.6g, Carbs: 5.3g, Protein: 6.2g

SPICY GRILLED VEGETABLES WITH A YOGURT & TAHINI DIP

Preparation time: 8 minutes | Cook time: 22 minutes | Servings: 2

Ingredients:

½ cup plain fat-free Greek-style yogurt

¼ teaspoon Spanish smoked paprika

2 Kaiser rolls

Fresh parsley, chopped

½ medium onion, quartered

1 (¾ lb.) eggplant, cut lengthwise into 4 wedges

½ head of radicchio, quartered

1 tomato, halved horizontally

6 large button mushrooms

2 tablespoons olive oil

½ teaspoon garlic, minced

¼ teaspoon salt, divided

¼ teaspoon ground cumin

¾ tablespoon tahini

½ tablespoon fresh lemon juice

Instructions:

1. Combine the yogurt, garlic, lemon juice, tahini, cumin, and ¼ teaspoon salt in a mixing bowl. Whisk until well combined then cover with plastic wrap and place in fridge.

2. In another mixing bowl, pour the oil and add the paprika. Whisk to combine.

3. Place the mushrooms, onion, tomato, eggplant, radicchio, and onion into bowl.

4. Pour the prepared paprika oil over the vegetables and toss until well coated.

5. Put the vegetables on the 1-inch cooking rack in a single layer.

6. Grill on "High" setting at 350°Fahrenheit for 22 minutes.

7. Around the 10-minute mark, open the dome and mix the vegetables around the bit.

8. Spoon the grilled vegetables onto a serving plate and serve with prepared yogurt and tahini sauce with Kaiser rolls.

Nutritional Information per serving:
Calories: 354, Total Fat: 4.3g, Carbs: 5.2g, Protein: 5.2g

TOFU, CHEESE & MARINARA SAUCE STUFFED BELL PEPPERS

Preparation time: 10 minutes | Cooking time: 24 minutes | Servings: 2

Ingredients:

½ cup brown rice

1 cup marinara sauce, divided

1 cup Mozzarella cheese, shredded

4 (1/2-inch) slices tomato

2 bell peppers, tops and seeds removed

½ (12-ounce) tofu, drained and diced

Instructions:

1. Follow the directions on package of rice.

2. Place the peppers in a baking dish.

3. Spoon about ¼ cup brown rice into each bell pepper.

4. Spoon about ½ cup of the marinara sauce over the layer of the brown rice and top with about ¼ cup mozzarella cheese each.

5. Divide the tofu equally between the two bell peppers and place over the layer of mozzarella cheese.

6. Place one slice of tomato on each bell pepper.

7. Sprinkle the remaining cheese over your bell peppers.

8. Cover the baking dish with a sheet of aluminum foil and bake on "High" setting at 325°Fahrenheit for 20 minutes.

9. Remove the foil and bake for an additional 4 minutes on "High" setting.

10. Serve hot with a side of your favorite condiment.

Nutritional Information per serving:

Calories: 341, Total Fat: 4.3g, Carbs: 4.6g, Protein: 5.6g

ARTICHOKE & FETA TORTILLA WRAPS WITH A YOGURT & CHIVE DIP

Preparation time: 10 minutes | Cook time: 15 minutes | Servings: 4

Ingredients:

½ (7-ounce) jar of sweet peppers, water drained and cut vertically

½ tablespoon chives, roughly chopped

½ (8-ounce) carton plain fat-free yogurt

4 whole tortillas (8-inch)

2 tablespoons pesto

2 tablespoons feta

⅔ cup parmesan, grated

¼ cup cream cheese

2 green onions, thinly chopped

½ (14-ounce) can artichoke hearts, drained and chopped finely

Instructions:

1. Grease an 8-inch by 8-inch silicone baking dish with cooking spray and set aside.
2. Place the artichoke hearts, feta cheese, green onions, cream cheese, parmesan, and pesto together in a mixing bowl. Mix well.
3. Place about 2 tablespoons of this mix on each tortilla.
4. Top the cream cheese mixture with red pepper strips.
5. Roll the tortilla into tight roll.
6. Place the tortilla rolls in the prepared silicone baking dish. Place the tortilla filled baking dish on the 3-inch cooking rack.
7. Cook on "High" setting at 342°Fahrenheit for about 15 minutes or until the tortillas are thoroughly heated.
8. While tortilla rolls heat through, prepare the dipping sauce.
9. Combine the chives and yogurt in a small mixing bowl and set aside.
10. Once cooked, cut the rolls in 3 parts and place on a serving plate.
11. Serve hot with the yogurt and chive dipping sauce on the side.

Nutritional Information per serving:

Calories: 335, Total Fat: 4.2g, Carbs: 4.7g, Protein: 5.2g

STREUSEL TOPPED BUTTERY SWEET POTATO CASSEROLE

Preparation time: 10 minutes | Cook time: 1 hour and 25 minutes | Servings: 3

Ingredients:

- 2 sweet potatoes
- 7 teaspoons flour, divided
- 2 tablespoons pecans, chopped
- ½ teaspoon vanilla
- 1 egg, slightly beaten
- ¼ teaspoon salt
- ¼ cup brown sugar

2/3 cup and 2 tablespoons butter

¼ cup sugar

Instructions:

1. Lightly fork the sweet potatoes and place them on the 3-inch rack.
2. Cook on "High" setting at 375°Fahrenheit for 45 minutes.
3. Remove the sweet potatoes from the oven and cool for 20 minutes.
4. Once cool enough to handle, peel the sweet potatoes.
5. Place the potatoes into a bowl and mash into a smooth pulp.
6. Add into the bowl 2/3 cup of butter, egg, vanilla, sugar, salt, and 1 teaspoon flour. Mix until well combined.
7. Pour the mixture into a 1-quart ovenproof casserole dish.
8. Place the casserole dish on the 1-inch rack.
9. Cook on the "High" setting for about 25 minutes.
10. While the casserole bakes, combine the remaining flour, leftover butter, pecans, and brown sugar together in mixing bowl. Mix well.
11. Once cook time is up, remove the dome and stir the casserole.
12. Pour the prepared streusel mix over the casserole in an even layer.
13. Continue baking on "High" setting at 342°Fahrenheit for 15 minutes. Serve hot.

Nutritional Information per serving:
Calories: 362, Total Fat: 4.1g, Carbs: 5.4g, Protein: 4.6g

PARMESAN CRUSTED ASPARAGUS SPEARS WITH BALSAMIC VINEGAR

Preparation time: 8 minutes | Cook time: 10 minutes | Servings: 3

Ingredients:

½ lb. asparagus

½ ounce parmesan cheese, shaved

½ tablespoon olive oil

2 tablespoons balsamic vinegar

Instructions:

1. Rinse the asparagus well and trim its ends.
2. Pour the olive oil over the asparagus spears and toss until well coated.
3. Spread the oil coated asparagus on the 3-inch cooking rack in a single layer.
4. Sprinkle the cheese over the asparagus and cook on "High" setting at 350°Fahrenheit for 10 minutes.
5. Remove the parmesan crusted asparagus spears to serving plate.
6. Pour the balsamic vinegar over the asparagus and serve immediately.

Nutritional Information per serving:
Calories: 352, Total Fat: 4.5g, Carbs: 5.2g, Protein: 4.7g

CHEESY ONION & ZUCCHINI AU GRATIN

Preparation time: 12 minutes | Cook time: 25 minutes | Servings: 2

Ingredients:

½ large yellow onion, cut into ½-inch pieces

¼ cup cheddar cheese, shredded

½ medium zucchini, cut into ½-inch slices

½ tablespoon olive oil

Instructions:

1. Place the yellow onion in a single layer in the liner pan and pour in the olive oil. Toss well.
2. Cook on "High" setting for 15 minutes, at 8-minute mark toss onions.
3. Place the zucchini slices over the onions.
4. Sprinkle with salt and pepper to taste.
5. Return the liner pan to the oven and cook on "High" setting at 342°Fahrenheit for 7 minutes. Sprinkle with cheese over the zucchini and cook for an additional 3 minutes. Serve hot.

Nutritional Information per serving:
Calories: 352, Total Fat: 3.6g, Carbs: 4.3g, Protein: 4.6g

ALMOND TOPPED CRUNCHY FRENCH BEANS

Preparation time: 10 minutes | Cook time: 17 minutes | Servings: 4

Ingredients:

- 6-ounces French green beans, trimmed and rinsed
- 1 tablespoon butter, melted
- ½ cup crispy onion ringlets, fried
- ¼ cup almonds, sliced
- 1 tablespoon olive oil
- 2 tablespoons lemon juice

Instructions:

1. Place the French beans in an ovenproof, 8-inch baking dish.
2. Pour the lemon juice and olive oil over the French beans and place into baking dish on the 1-inch cooking rack.
3. Cook on the "High" setting at 325°Fahrenheit for 12 minutes.
4. Sprinkle the almonds and onions over the beans and continue to cook for an additional 5 minutes on "High" setting. Serve immediately.

Nutritional Information per serving:

Calories: 364, Total Fat: 10.2g, Carbs: 6.2g, Protein: 5.2g

MAYONNAISE & CHEESE COVERED CORN

Preparation time: 8 minutes | Cook time: 20 minutes | Servings: 8

Ingredients:

- 4 ears of corn, cut into 4 pieces each
- ½ cup mayonnaise
- 16 lime wedges
- Salt and pepper to taste
- Fresco, grated
- Chili powder or paprika to taste

1 cup Queso cheese, grated

½ cup melted butter

Instructions:

1. Place the corncob pieces on the 3-inch rack.
2. Grill on the "High" setting at 375°Fahrenheit for about 10-minutes on each side.
3. Remove the corncobs from the oven and pour butter over each piece.
4. Pour the mayonnaise on the corn.
5. Sprinkle with cheese, salt, pepper, paprika, over corn pieces.
6. Serve hot with lime wedges on the side.

Nutritional Information per serving:

Calories: 351, Total Fat: 4.3g, Carbs: 5.2g, Protein: 5.7g

BAKED TOMATO & CHEESE CASSEROLE

Preparation time: 12 minutes | Cook time: 20 minutes | Servings: 2

Ingredients:

2 tablespoons olive oil, divided

5 basil leaves, thinly sliced and divided

Salt and black pepper to taste

½ tablespoon parmesan cheese, shredded

½ tablespoon melted butter

4 mini fresh mozzarella balls, cut into quarters (1/4 cup)

1 tablespoon olive oil

1 clove garlic, minced

½ (14-ounce) can diced tomatoes, drained

½ cup breadcrumbs

½ (14-ounce) can whole plum tomatoes, peeled and drained

Instructions:

1. Place the breadcrumbs and 1 tablespoon olive oil mixed together in mixing bowl. Toss and combine well, then set aside.

2. Pour the remaining olive oil into a mixing bowl.

3. Add the plum tomatoes, diced tomatoes, garlic, mozzarella, butter, parmesan cheese, basil leaves, salt, and pepper and mix well.

4. Grease an 8-inch by 8-inch baking dish with remaining olive oil.

5. Pour the prepared cheese and tomato mix into baking dish.

6. Top with the prepared breadcrumb mixture.

7. Place baking dish on the 1-inch cooking rack and bake at 350° Fahrenheit for 20 minutes. Serve hot.

Nutritional Information per serving:
Calories: 362, Total Fat: 5.2g, Carbs: 4.3g, Protein: 5.1g

RICOTTA & STUFFED JUMBO PASTA SHELLS

Preparation time: 8 minutes | Cook time: 17 minutes | Servings: 6

Ingredients:

6 jumbo pasta shells, cooked

½ teaspoon Italian seasoning

½ (26-ounce) jar spaghetti sauce, divided

Salt and black pepper to taste

½ egg, slightly beaten

5 ounces sautéed spinach

1 cup ricotta cheese

¼ cup parmesan cheese, shredded, divided

Instructions:

1. Place the ricotta cheese into a large mixing bowl. Add in about 2 tablespoons of parmesan, egg, pepper, salt, spinach, and Italian seasoning.

2. Mix until ingredients are well combined.

3. Spoon the prepared mixture into the cooked jumbo pasta shells.

4. Spread the 6 tablespoons of spaghetti sauce into the bottom of a baking pan about 4-inch by 4-inch.

5. Place the ricotta and spinach stuffed shells in the baking pan.

6. Pour the remaining spaghetti sauce over the pasta shells and top with the remaining 2 tablespoons parmesan cheese.

7. Place the baking pan on the 1-inch cooking rack and bake for about 17 minutes at 375° Fahrenheit. Serve hot.

Nutritional Information per serving:
Calories: 343, Total Fat: 4.5g, Carbs: 4.3g, Protein: 5.1g

CHIVE TOPPED POTATOES

Preparation time: 6 minutes | Cook time: 40 minutes | Servings: 1

Ingredients:

1 medium russet potato, washed and cut into ⅛-inch slices

Fresh ground black pepper and salt to taste

1 ½ tablespoons butter, melted

Instructions:

1. Add about ½ teaspoon of butter to the bottom of an 8-inch baking pan. Swirl the butter around to grease the bottom of the pan.

2. Place the potato slices in the greased baking pan in a spiral pattern, starting from the outside and working towards the center.

3. Brush some butter onto potato slices and sprinkle with salt and pepper to taste.

4. Repeat steps 2 and 3 until all the potato slices have been arranged in the pan.

5. Place the prepared pan on the 1-inch cooking rack.

6. Cook on "High" power setting at 375°Fahrenheit for about 40 minutes.

Nutritional Information per serving:
Calories: 346, Total Fat: 4.2g, Carbs: 4.3g, Protein: 5.3g

Chapter 7
__Desserts__

BERRY CREAM PIE

Preparation time: 12 minutes | Cook time: 55 minutes | Servings: 18

Ingredients:

   1 teaspoon almond extract

   2 cups sugar

   12 ounces fresh raspberries

   12 ounces fresh blackberries

   2 lbs. fresh strawberries, sliced or chopped

   1 teaspoon vanilla extract

   2 unbaked pastry shells (10 inches each)

   2 cups sour cream

Instructions:

1. Prick the pastry shells with a fork in various places on the bottom as well as the sides.

2. Place the pastry on the 2-inch rack and bake on power level "High" at 325° Fahrenheit for 15 minutes. When done, cool completely.

3. Meanwhile, add sugar, salt, vanilla, almond extract, and sour cream into a bowl. Mix until well combined.

4. Gently fold in the berries. Divide the berry mixture between the two crusts.

5. Attach an extender ring to the base tray.

6. Bake on power setting "8" for 45 minutes. Bake in batches if needed.

7. Remove from oven and cool on wire rack.

8. Place in the fridge for a couple of hours before serving. Slice into wedges and serve.

Nutritional Information per serving:

Calories: 324, Total Fat: 6.4g, Carbs: 8.7g, Protein: 10.3g

GOLDEN CAKE

Preparation time: 15 minutes | Cook time: 30 minutes | Servings: 8

Ingredients:

2 boxes of super moist yellow cake mix

For icing:

4 containers of Betty Crocker Rich and Creamy chocolate icing

Instructions:

1. Make the cake batter according to the cake box recipe instructions.

2. Grease 2 large cake pans with cooking spray.

3. Divide and pour the batter into the cake pans.

4. Place on 1-inch rack in your NuWave Oven and place a dish on the rack. Bake in batches if needed.

5. Attach an extender ring to the base of the tray.

6. Bake on power level "8" and set the timer for 30 minutes.

7. Take your cake out of the oven and place on a wire rack to cool.

8. Ice the cake according to the instructions on the container.

Nutritional Information per serving:

Calories: 463, Total Fat: 13.4g, Carbs: 10.2g, Protein: 6.2g

BLUEBERRY STREUSEL COFFEE CAKE

Preparation time: 12 minutes | Cook time: 30 minutes | Servings: 20

Ingredients:

2 cups blueberries, fresh or frozen

1 cup milk

½ teaspoon salt

2 cups pecans, chopped

1 cup butter, softened

2 eggs

4 teaspoons baking powder

4 cups + 6 tablespoons all-purpose flour

For streusel topping:

1 cup sugar

½ cup cold butter, chopped into small pieces

1 cup flour

Instructions:

1. To make streusel topping: add the sugar and flour into mixing bowl. Mix well. Add the butter and mix until a crumbly mixture has formed. Set aside.

2. To make the cake: mix the flour, sugar, salt, and baking powder in a bowl.

3. Add the eggs, butter, and milk. Beat with electric mixer until you have a smooth batter.

4. Add the pecans and blueberries and fold gently. Pour the batter into a large greased spring form baking pan. Sprinkle streusel topping over it.

5. Attach an extender ring to the base of the tray.

6. Bake on power level "8" for 30 minutes.

7. Remove from the oven and cool for some time.

8. Slice and serve warm.

Nutritional Information per serving:

Calories: 412, Total Fat: 14.2g, Carbs: 9.2g, Protein: 8.2g

RASPBERRY CRUMBLE

Preparation time: 10 minutes | Cook time: 20 minutes | Servings: 8

Ingredients:

1 cup unsalted butter, softened

½ cup cornstarch

4 pints fresh raspberries

3 cups brown sugar

Juice of 4 lemons

2 cups all-purpose flour

Instructions:

1. Add brown sugar, butter, and flour into a mixing bowl. Mix well using your hands until it has a crumbly texture.

2. In another bowl add the rest of the ingredients.

3. Take 8 ramekins. Divide the mixture among the ramekins. Sprinkle the flour mixture over the raspberry mixture.

4. Place ramekins on the 2-inch rack and attach extender ring to the base tray.

5. Bake on "High" power level at 342° Fahrenheit for 20 minutes.

6. Remove from oven and cool, then serve.

Nutritional Information per serving:

Calories: 423, Total Fat: 13.2g, Carbs: 12.2g, Protein: 6.2g

PUMPKIN COOKIE SANDWICHES WITH CREAM CHEESE FILLING

Preparation time: 12 minutes | Cook time: 15 minutes | Servings: 12

Ingredients:

½ cup olive oil

1 large egg

½ teaspoon baking soda

1 ½ cups all-purpose flour

½ teaspoon salt

½ teaspoon baking powder

½ teaspoon vanilla extract

½ tablespoon pumpkin pie spice

½ cup pumpkin puree

1 cup light brown sugar

Cream cheese filling:

1 (4-ounce package) cream cheese, softened

1 teaspoon pure vanilla extract

½ cup butter softened

2 ¼ cups powdered sugar

Instructions to Make the Cookies:

1. Grease the liner pan with some butter or cooking spray.

2. Place the brown sugar and olive oil in a bowl. Beat with electric beater until smooth.

3. Add your egg and continue beating until the egg is well combined into the mix.

4. Add in the pumpkin puree, vanilla, baking soda, pumpkin pie spice, baking powder, and salt. Continue to whisk until it is light and fluffy.

5. Slowly fold using a rubber spatula. Do not over mix or batter will fall flat.

6. Use a small cookie spoon or a round tablespoon and scoop the batter into the greased liner pan. Leave about 2-inches between cookies.

7. Place the extender ring on the base of your NuWave Oven and cover the dome.

8. Cook on "High" setting at 342° Fahrenheit for 15 minutes.

9. Allow the cookies to cool completely before filling them with the cream cheese filling.

Instructions to Make the Cream Cheese Filling:

1. Add the cream cheese and butter in the bowl of an electric mixer.

2. Cream the butter and cream cheese together on medium speed. Stop the mixer at regular intervals so that you can scrape the side of the bowl.

3. Add your vanilla and continue whisking for another few minutes.

4. Lower the speed of the electric mixer and gradually add the powdered sugar to the cream cheese and butter mix.

5. Continue beating until mix is light and fluffy.

6. Spoon the cream cheese filling on the flat side of cooled cookies. Take another cookie and place it on top and gently press down lightly. Serve immediately.

Nutritional Information per serving:

Calories: 422, Total Fat: 14.2, Carbs: 9.2g, Protein: 8.2g

Conclusion

I hope you and your loved ones spend many a meal based on this collection of NuWave Oven recipes. They are not only a tasty selection of recipes, but they include healthy ingredients that will certainly make you feel good when serving them to your friends and family. I am sure they will be asking you to whip up their favorite NuWave Oven recipes in no time! Enjoy your new appliance that will make things that much easier for you when it comes to preparing your daily meals. In this fast-paced world we live in today, using an appliance like the NuWave Oven will make meal times in your household pleasant! Happy cooking with your NuWave Oven. Hopefully this collection of recipes will help get you on your way to perfecting cooking with your NuWave Oven!

Made in United States
North Haven, CT
29 May 2025

69305208R00057